Christopher Murray is an A   at University College, Dublin. His pub   include *Twentieth-Century Irish Drama: Mirror Up to a Nation* (Manchester, 1997) and *Brian Friel: Essays, Diaries, Interviews 1964–1999* (Faber, 1999)

Bill Naismith, the series editor of the Faber Critical Guides, was a Lecturer in Drama at the University of London, Goldsmiths' College, for twenty-five years and now lectures in drama for the Central University of Iowa in London. His other published work includes Student Guides to *'Top Girls' by Caryl Churchill* (Methuen, 1991), *'The Rover' by Aphra Behn* (Methuen, 1993), *'Across Oka' by Robert Holman* (Methuen, 1994) and *'Our Country's Good' by Timberlake Wertenbaker* (Methuen, 1995).

A FABER CRITICAL GUIDE
Sean O'Casey

The Shadow of a Gunman
Juno and the Paycock
The Plough and the Stars

CHRISTOPHER MURRAY

faber and faber
LONDON·NEW YORK

First published in 2000
by Faber and Faber Limited
3 Queen Square London WC1N 3AU
Published in the United States by Faber and Faber Inc.,
an affiliate of Farrar, Straus and Giroux, New York

Photoset by Wilmaset Ltd, Birkenhead, Wirral
Printed in England by Mackays of Chatham plc, Chatham, Kent

A CIP record for this book
is available from the British Library
ISBN 0-571-19780-9

2 4 6 8 10 9 7 5 3 1

Contents

Editor's Preface

The *Faber Critical Guides* provide comprehensive introductions to major dramatists of the twentieth century.

The need to make an imaginative leap when reading dramatic texts is well known. Plays are written with live performance in mind. Often a theatre audience is confronted with a stage picture, a silent character or a vital movement – any of which might be missed in a simple 'reading'. The *Guides* advise you what to look for.

All plays emerge from a context – a background – the significance of which may vary but needs to be appreciated if the original impact of the play is to be understood. A writer may be challenging convention, reacting to the social and political life of the time or engaging with intellectual ideas. The *Guides* provide coverage of the appropriate context in each case.

A number of key texts are examined in each *Guide* in order to provide a sound introduction to the individual dramatists. Studying only one work is rarely enough to make informed judgements about the style and originality of a writer's work. Considering several plays is also the only way to follow a writer's development.

Finally, the *Guides* are meant to be read in conjunction with the play texts. 'The play's the thing' and must always be the primary concern. Not only are all playwrights different but every play has its own distinctive features which the *Guides* are concerned to highlight.

Note on References

Page references to *The Shadow of a Gunman*, *Juno and the Paycock* and *The Plough and the Stars* are to the texts as published in *Sean O'Casey: Three Dublin Plays*, London: Faber and Faber, 1998.

The full titles and publication details of the writings of Sean O'Casey and other critical works to which references are made throughout this book are given at the end of the relevant chapters.

Introduction

There are some writers whose personalities and life-histories are so attractive that we find ourselves drawn to them and captivated even before taking their work into account. Sean O'Casey was one of those writers. An underdog all his life and without benefit of more than the most basic education, O'Casey spoke out loudly and often on all matters to do with human rights. Born into poverty, his sympathies lay always with the poor and the underprivileged. He became not only a playwright of the people but a constant commentator, in letters to the newspapers and in articles for magazines, on injustices of every kind. Indeed, it would hardly be too much to say that O'Casey's whole life and career were dedicated to opposing injustice wherever and whenever he saw it.

But every writer is governed and moulded by the time and place in which he or she was born and brought up. When O'Casey was born in Dublin on 30 March 1880, that city was still a British colony ruled from Westminster. As a Protestant, O'Casey (or as his name was before he gave it a Gaelic spelling, 'John Casey') was automatically unionist in politics. Even though working class (Michael Casey was a clerk), the Casey family saw themselves as apart from the Roman Catholic majority, who were for the most part nationalists in favour of Home Rule for Ireland. O'Casey might have settled himself comfortably into lower-middle-class Dublin life by using the advantages of his Protestant connections, even though, being poor, he lacked the privileges which allowed fellow-Dubliners Synge and Wilde to attend Dublin University (Trinity College); to be Protestant in Dublin one hundred years ago was at least to be on the winning side. But poverty, especially after his father's death when the boy was only six years old, and the eye disease trachoma seriously stunted O'Casey's development. He had only three years' education up to the age of fourteen, but benefited from his older sister Bella's qualifications as a teacher. After that, while working on and off in lowly jobs in Dublin businesses in his teenage years, O'Casey educated himself by reading all the books he could lay his hands on and which his painful eyesight would allow him to study. In particular, he steeped himself in the Bible – a requirement of his Sunday-school class – and Shakespeare (O'Casey's brother was a part-time actor). Finding that Dublin libraries were ill-stocked in the materials which interested him most, O'Casey formed the habit of buying cheap editions of the great authors in the second-hand bookstores. A love of learning, often the most powerful fuel of the would-be writer, was thus early fostered. Ever afterwards O'Casey was a voracious reader, not just in dramatic literature (where Shaw became a favourite alongside Shakespeare) but in poetry, religious studies, art and music. It is no surprise that the characters in his plays to whom O'Casey is most sympathetic are usually those, like Mary Boyle in *Juno and the Paycock*, who strive to lift themselves out of a restrictive environment through reading. Later in life, O'Casey wrote essays on the writers he most admired: Shakespeare, Ibsen, Gorki, Shaw, Synge, Yeats, and many more. The view he adhered to all his life was that books were for all, not just for the educated, and that they were as important to the working person as bread on the table.

When regular office employment of any kind proved impossible for O'Casey (mainly because he could not put up with the grovelling to authority it seemed to require) he took up hard manual labour with the Dublin railways. He enjoyed the outdoor work with pick and shovel but when he insisted on his right to join a trade union in 1911 he was dismissed. From that time on, until his plays began to make money, O'Casey could get work only occasionally, and he lived a simple hard life with his mother Susan on little more than her old-age pension until she died in November 1918. He then set about making his living as a writer, first of popular verse, then as historian of the Irish Citizen Army (which had fought without his help in the 1916 Rising) and eventually, from 1923, as a playwright for the Abbey Theatre in Dublin. Once his plays proved successful enough to be accepted in London he went to live there and never again worked at anything else but full-time writing.

The rejection by the Abbey Theatre of his anti-war play *The Silver Tassie* in 1928 led O'Casey into more experimental work. It is often said that the break with the Abbey, where he had learned his trade, was tragic for O'Casey; in any event, although *Within the Gates* (1934) and *The Star Turns Red* (1940) were brave experiments, these and other later plays were not successful on the London stage. By this time O'Casey was fully committed to Communism, although never a member of the party, and this commitment increasingly told against him. His first biographer, David Krause, has described O'Casey as 'a moral pacifist as well as a militant socialist', and this accurately sums up O'Casey's political position. It is little wonder that when the English theatre underwent a revolution in 1956 and angry new writers emerged, they showed their admiration for O'Casey by writing in a somewhat similar, realistic but anti-establishment mode. There was thus a renewal of interest in O'Casey's plays around 1960, by which time he was eighty years old and close to death. So far as most critics of modern drama are concerned, O'Casey's best work was complete with *The Plough and the Stars*, written almost forty years before his death in Torquay, Devon, in September 1964. But he himself always insisted that his later, experimental, plays were better.

While waiting for his new plays to win acceptance in the 1930s, O'Casey began an autobiography which exceeded his modest expectations by growing into six enormously popular books. Works of art in their own right, several of the books relate directly or indirectly to the Dublin plays. For background to the social and political conditions of Ireland before and after 1916, the reader will be well repaid to look into *Drums under the Windows* (1945, Book 3 of the autobiography) and *Inishfallen, Fare Thee Well* (1949, Book 4).

The kind of play which interested O'Casey and which he slowly managed to write was a mixture of Shakespeare and melodrama. In one of his later plays, *Red Roses for Me* (1943), he makes the autobiographical hero, about to play a scene in *Henry VI, Part 3*, comment on how the working class are afraid of Shakespeare because of his overwhelming reputation. 'They think he's beyond them, while all the time he's part of the kingdom of heaven in the nature of everyman.' O'Casey admired Shakespeare for the vividness of characterisation, as well as for the incomparably rich language and buoyant rhythm. But being a committed political activist, O'Casey also admired how Shakespeare managed to combine the treatment of war, civil war and political power-struggles with the requirements of entertainment. The plays of the Irish melodramatist Dion Boucicault (1820–90) were another useful influence. As a teenager O'Casey had played the part of Father Dolan in *The Shaughraun* (1874), a mixture of songs, romantic love and political adventure set in Ireland at the time of the Fenian rebellion. O'Casey saw that this balance between politics and entertainment was vital. However, it took him some time to achieve it. His early plays written for the Abbey have all but one been lost, yet this play, *The Harvest Festival* (never performed) shows what a long way he had yet to go. It is a play about a workers' strike, too full of argument and propaganda, influenced by the plays of Shaw. O'Casey had certainly read and admired Shaw's work by this time (1919), for he actually wrote to ask Shaw if he would write a preface to a book of political essays. Shaw refused, telling O'Casey to go his own way, and in fact the book was never published. O'Casey found Shaw's advice valuable and the two men became friends. O'Casey had to learn for himself how to deal better with a political subject or situation within a play. He thus worked out a mixture of comedy and political commentary for *The Shadow of a Gunman*, the first play of his to be accepted by the Abbey.

The material of the three Dublin plays owes a lot to O'Casey's experience as a young man involved in Irish political and cultural life. From about 1906 he was a member of the Gaelic League where he learned the Irish language, first changed his name, and became fiercely nationalistic. He joined the Irish Republican Brotherhood not long afterwards and rejoiced in writing anti-British propaganda. But when Jim Larkin (1882–1947) arrived in

Dublin from Liverpool and set about creating an active trade union movement, O'Casey began to abandon all religious, cultural and republican organisations in favour of socialism. The great lock-out of 1913, which saw thousands of Dublin manual workers in opposition to the bosses controlling the transport and distribution industries and services, showed O'Casey that the cause of labour took precedence over the cause of Irish freedom. He was appointed secretary of the Irish Citizen Army which Larkin formed in 1914 for the defence of the workers and for a while he was active in administration. But, characteristically, he was unable to reconcile his own views with those of the majority and resigned in 1914 on a policy matter. O'Casey was thus isolated by the time of the 1916 Easter Rising. He became a spectator of Irish political life when he might have been a major participant.

The 1916 Rising, led by Pádraic Pearse (Commandant, Irish Volunteers) and James Connolly (Commandant, Irish Citizen Army), was an abortive one. It took place in some confusion on Easter Monday 1916 following an attempt by the chief of staff of the Irish Volunteers (Eoin MacNeill) to cancel the proceedings. Pearse and Connolly, in defiance of MacNeill, led a revolt which failed to spread outside the city of Dublin. No more than 2,000 men in all participated, taking over the General Post Office and other strategic sites in Dublin. This heroic but foolhardy undertaking, marred by indecision, poor communications, lack of firepower, and lack of general support, was easily crushed by British forces within a week. Pearse, Connolly and thirteen other leaders were summarily executed. It was these executions which changed the political climate in Ireland and precipitated the guerilla war of independence which led to the signing of the Treaty between Britain and Ireland in 1921, and the establishment of a twenty-six-county Free State in the South.

O'Casey, while admiring the courage of those who fought in 1916, saw the enterprise as a waste of life and effort. In particular, he faulted Connolly for deflecting the cause of labour into a nationalist struggle. By making an alliance between the Irish Citizen Army and the Irish Volunteers under Pearse, Connolly had, in O'Casey's analysis, betrayed the true purpose of the Irish Citizen Army and taken part in a charade. He makes this point in his *Story of the Irish Citizen Army* (1919). O'Casey's attitude towards the Rising, then, tended to be critical and condemnatory. By this time, and especially after the 1917 Russian Revolution (which he applauded), nationalism was for him a delusion.

This was not always the case. His early writings, journalistic pieces and poems, were unashamedly republican in theme and language. After 1913 his writings became more socialist than nationalist but were still propagandist in style. It is indeed remarkable that such a fanatic as O'Casey's early writings show him to have been (as evidenced in the collection of his early work entitled *Feathers from the Green Crow*) should ever have grown into a major dramatic artist. There is something miraculous about this shift in direction, though 'fate' and O'Casey's character no doubt were other factors. But the three Dublin plays are like the great war poems written by Owen, Sassoon and others: they would not have anything like their impact and intensity were it not for the authors' personal and complex experience, which rendered them pacifist in outlook.

Although O'Casey's first loves were Shakespeare and Boucicault, his plays are distinctively modern. He takes his place among the post-Ibsenist dramatists dedicated to mirroring the conditions of modern life. But whereas Ibsen, and indeed his contemporaries Strindberg and Chekhov, concentrated on the middle-class world, the so-called 'pillars of society', for their material, O'Casey chose the tenement life he knew best. In terms of dramatic form he was uncomfortable with realism and its more extreme version, naturalism. But as an Abbey playwright he more or less adopted realism as a matter of course.

Distinctively, his plays are much freer in structure than the three-act realistic play usually demands: O'Casey prefers to work from life, combining a scanty plot with character sketches with 'turns' reminiscent of the music-hall. At times O'Casey's use of the group, the ensemble, in preference to the individual hero, is reminiscent of Chekhov's style, for example in *Three Sisters* (1901). But O'Casey's world, the world he creates on stage, is vastly different from Chekhov's, which is invariably sophistic-ated, intellectually advanced, and poised ready to fall apart. O'Casey's is a more robust, devil-may-care, down-to-earth world, where the working-class characters struggle to survive. O'Casey abolishes the hero in favour of the anti-hero. In doing so, he introduces a good deal of irony and even satire into the dramatic action.

O'Casey extended the Irish tradition in ways which were to affect how the modern theatre developed. The Abbey players who brought his plays on to the London and New York stages in the late 1920s and early 1930s were among the best of their generation and included Barry Fitzgerald, Sara Allgood and F. J. McCormick. Their ensemble-playing held lessons for repertories all over the world. Also, the plays themselves, in their combination of tragedy and comedy to form a new and modern tragicomedy, pointed the way for many twentieth-century writers from Osborne to Bond. These later writers looked back with great respect to O'Casey's pioneering work, for they too were trying to find ways of using the stage to combine entertainment and criticism of social and political values. Beckett, whose political outlook was as different from O'Casey's as his Dublin origins, nevertheless admired and may even have imitated O'Casey's use of knockabout farce within the tragic situation.

As time passed, O'Casey's three Dublin plays became part of the world repertoire of twentieth-century drama. Indeed, opinion elevated Sir Laurence Olivier's 1966 production of *Juno* at the National Theatre in London into one of the best ever seen. Further, the representation of the long-suffering mother, Juno, was to be imitated by many playwrights, including the American Clifford Odets and the British Arnold Wesker. O'Casey's depiction of warfare, particularly in its urban, guerilla aspects, showed many other writers how best to dramatise politics: by uniting simple home or domestic life with the world of political violence. This link between private and public was the means of showing cause and effect and how people's lives can be torn apart by the forces which invade and conflict with their happy, careless routines.

Finally, it needs to be emphasised that O'Casey, far from being a narrow, politically biased playwright, always shows the deepest compassion for the sufferings of his characters. Indeed, it would not be too much to say that O'Casey's plays, while dealing with issues of life and death, are invariably and enthusiastically on the side of life.

References

Krause, David, 'The Maiming of Sean O'Casey', *Sean O'Casey Review*, ed. Robert Lowery, 3.2 (Spring 1977), p. 137.

O'Casey, Sean, *The Autobiographies*, 6 books, published in 2 vols., London: Macmillan, 1963.

– *Red Roses for Me*, in *Sean O'Casey: Plays One*, London: Faber and Faber, 1998.

Context and Background

The theatre for which O'Casey first wrote was the Abbey in Dublin. Founded in 1904 by the poet W. B. Yeats (1865–1939), the playwright and administrator Lady Gregory (1852–1932) and the poet and playwright John Millington Synge (1871–1909), the Abbey from the outset was a brave and combative little theatre. Its origins lay in two impulses which were not always in harmony and when in opposition created explosive audience reaction. One impulse was to create a theatre of art along the lines of the new 'free' or 'independent' theatres in London, Paris, Berlin and, perhaps most famously, Moscow. There was a common idea stretching right across Europe from the late 1880s, namely to oppose the commercial, conventional theatre of the nineteenth century, with its star system, its reliance on spectacular scenery and sensational effects to create the maximum illusion, and its cultivation of worn-out dramatic styles (as seen in the 'well-made play' in particular). The Independent Theatre established in London in 1891 probably first gave Yeats the idea of providing an alternative theatre for Dublin, where similar conditions were in place. Indeed, Yeats himself contributed an early play to the Independent Theatre in 1894, sharing the double bill with Shaw's *Arms and the Man*. Shaw, however, was a lot more interested in using the Independent Theatre to create a new drama similar to the realistic plays of Ibsen (1828–1906), such as *A Doll's House* (1879) and *Ghosts* (1881). Yeats was rather more interested in Symbolism, and in the new poetic plays he had seen or read in Paris. He had serious doubts about the value of realism, and hoped to control its development in favour of a restoration of poetic drama to the stage. However, the spread of naturalism – an extreme form of realism – across Europe culminated in the establishment in 1898 of the Moscow Art Theatre, dedicated to the plays of Anton Chekhov (1860–1904). One of the founders of the MAT, Constantin Stanislavsky, quickly developed acting and staging techniques to make Chekhov's plays seem more real and more natural than anything seen in the theatre before.

Naturalism thus conquered the older nineteenth-century theatre of illusionism. The Moscow Art Theatre merely brought to perfection certain revolutionary developments already challenging the older styles and traditions and paved the way for the triumph of realism. Yeats, it has to be said, was somewhat dismayed by this victory and did not in fact accept it. At the Abbey he fought to maintain a theatre movement which had two strands: poetic drama (mainly written by himself) and realistic 'peasant plays' (best written by J. M. Synge) which owed a lot to the new naturalistic ideas on authenticity of setting, costume and acting style.

As time went on, the realistic side of the Abbey repertory seemed to win out over the poetic or symbolic. And yet it could be said that the Abbey plays, such as Synge's *Riders to the Sea* (1903) or Lady Gregory's *Spreading the News* (1904), were not realistic in the same way as, for example, Shaw's *Candida* (1895) or *Major Barbara* (1906). The Abbey plays usually had a remote, other-worldly flavour and did not seem directly to relate to the events and problems of contemporary life. After the premature death of Synge in 1909, however, others began to write more sordid, more genuinely realistic plays. Writers such as Lennox Robinson (1886–1958) and T. C. Murray (1873–1959) held the mirror up to disillusioned Irish life in the style of Ibsen's problem plays. Yeats, having abandoned the Abbey for the moment in order to write poetic plays modelled on the Japanese Noh drama in London, seemed about to give up the fight against realism in Dublin. He wrote a famous open letter to Lady Gregory in 1919: 'we did not set out to create this sort of theatre, and its success has been to me a discouragement and a defeat.' And yet, if Yeats could have been fair about this point, Abbey realism had already created some of the most striking and original work in the modern theatre, and was about to recreate former glories in the new drama of Sean O'Casey.

The second impulse was nationalism. Here the Abbey Theatre was quite unlike any other of the new little theatres in London, Paris, Berlin or Moscow, all of which concentrated on fighting the existing commercial theatres with a new set of artistic principles. The new Irish theatre complicated matters by making its foundation part of the movement in cultural nationalism which thrived in Dublin and elsewhere in Ireland from the early 1890s. The literary renaissance which then developed, headed by Yeats, celebrated independence as the goal worth fighting for. Home Rule seemed a real possibility as time went on, but there was a group of militant republicans (of whom Maud Gonne, Yeats's lover, was one) whose extremism penetrated all activities. These nationalists assumed that the Abbey Theatre, which was built on their support, had a duty to idealise Ireland first and be entertaining or satirical only when the consciousness-raising was accomplished. Therefore, when Synge began to write comedies which, far from idealising Ireland or Irish manners, actually held them up to some ridicule, the nationalist critics and supporters turned on 'their' theatre and demanded Synge's head. Yeats was determined to fight for artistic freedom, even where the artist took it upon him or herself to laugh at flaws and absurdities in Irish life. He answered the journalist and founder of Sinn Féin Arthur Griffith in 1905 by insisting that Synge had heard the story of *The Shadow of the Glen* (1903) on the Aran Islands and not in Paris as Griffith, accusing Synge of French decadence, had said in his newspaper. Yeats was clearly arguing that Synge was being faithful to what he saw and heard among the people, and, according to Yeats's own definition in 'First Principles' (1904), national literature 'is the work of writers who are moulded by influences that are moulding their country, and who write out of so deep a life that they are accepted there in the end'. Synge's case was to be O'Casey's later on.

But first came the storm over Synge's *The Playboy of the Western World* in January 1907, which uncannily anticipated the riots that greeted *The Plough and the Stars* in February 1926. Synge's play, a comedy and a satire, greatly angered that section of the Abbey's audience who were either strong nationalists or members of the urban Catholic middle class, who resented this slur, as they saw it, on Irish rural people. In a programme note, Synge claimed once again that his play was based on reality ('suggested by an actual occurrence in the West') and that the language was also devised from the speech of the people. In short, he claimed *The Playboy* was realism. But its first audience took exception to what they saw and heard on patriotic grounds; in painting the people as fools, worshippers of a murderer, and (worst of all) immoral, this play *must* be a sneer at the 'real' Irish. Lady Gregory and Synge had to send a telegram to Yeats, who was lecturing in Scotland: 'Audience broke up in disorder at the word shift'. The reference was to Christy Mahon's speech, 'It's Pegeen I'm seeking only, and what'd I care if you brought me a drift of chosen females, standing in their shifts [underwear] itself, maybe, from this place to the eastern world?' The police were called in the next night, and the play went on amid uproar, the actors playing 'almost entirely in dumb show'. When Yeats returned on the next day he took over and determined to fight back in defence of artistic freedom. That night the police were there again, and many arrests were made. Yeats shouted at the audience his determination that *The Playboy* would not be taken off. And so it went, night after night, with up to fifty policemen in the aisles of the Abbey and opposition continuing. The play completed its short run and then Yeats arranged a public debate at the Abbey – to which Synge himself did not come. Yeats made one of his bravest speeches to a hostile audience; when they refused to listen he reminded them that he was the author of the patriotic play *Cathleen Ni Houlihan*.

The story of the *Playboy* riots makes clear the principles on which the Abbey was run. As a modern theatre, established as an alternative to commercialism, it was dedicated to forms of entertainment which are fundamentally artistic and truth-telling. As a theatre founded in the midst of a nationalist movement it was supposed to hold a mirror to the realities of Irish experience and of Irish history. But above all it stood for the writer: the Abbey was primarily a writers' theatre and an actors' theatre after that. And the writer had to be free to cultivate his or her vision of Ireland, regardless of propaganda.

O'Casey ran into exactly the same problems at the Abbey as Synge. However, it has to be said that O'Casey was more politicised. When he wrote *The Story of the Irish Citizen Army* (1919), an account of how Larkin's army formed, O'Casey had become somewhat disillusioned with Irish nationalism. But from the sidelines, as it were, he observed and continued to observe the factions which, after 1916, gradually united under the Sinn Féin umbrella and left Labour in the lurch. The flag of the ICA was the 'starry plough', representing the labourers toiling to reach the stars (i.e., some kind of spiritual fulfilment built upon their manual labour). To O'Casey, the 'plough and the stars' represented a struggle which should have been directed solely at the improvement of the workers' conditions. Hence his impatience with the blood-sacrifice of 1916. O'Casey further argued that after 1918 Irish Labour 'will probably have to fight Sinn Féin ... but the labour leaders must become wiser and more broadminded than they at present seem to be' if they were to democratise the national movement.

Beginning with *The Shadow of a Gunman* (1923), O'Casey introduced a new form of realism to the Abbey Theatre. Because he could not afford the price of admission, he had been to the Abbey only twice before his own plays were staged there. One of the plays he saw was *Blight* (1918), a little-known drama by Oliver St John Gogarty which for the first time introduced the Dublin slums onto the stage. Here poverty, consumption and appalling living conditions 'blight' the lives of the ordinary Dublin characters. O'Casey's outlook was never so bleak or pessimistic, and he was always eager to contextualise his representations politically; that is, to locate his stories of tenement life within the political events and atmosphere of the day. This concern lent to O'Casey's plays their special distinction. Each play juxtaposes two worlds, the private and the public. The private is the life of the tenement dwellers, where indeed privacy is hardly to be thought of: and yet the families who encroach freely on each other's space are preoccupied with personal and domestic problems. The public life in O'Casey's plays inevitably means the political: he shows how the affairs of state and the ambitions of freedom hold the lives of ordinary people in a vice. There is no escape from the battles raging in the streets. There is no hiding place from the consequences of a movement dedicated to overthrowing the oppressor. O'Casey's point of view is neither nationalist nor unionist: on balance it is anti-unionist and anti-imperialist, but it is the 'balance' which matters. Compassion takes precedence over political allegiance or ideology; each of the three Dublin plays is called a 'tragedy'. The laws of tragedy insist that pity and terror rather than political ideas should be primary. O'Casey's great achievement was to rise above local allegiances and turn the harsh conditions of working-class life into the materials of modern art.

It was stated above that the Abbey Theatre was and remains a writers' theatre first and an actors' second. Yet this is not to deny the contribution of the Abbey actors to the playwrights' achievements. From the beginning, the Abbey actors avoided the 'star system' dominant in the English and French theatres (whereby a production was mainly if not solely for the performances of some major actor or actress, while all other performers were supposed to keep out of the 'limelight' and subordinate their talents to the star's). The Abbey style is based on the ensemble, which means that no one individual gets top billing; all actors are regarded as equal. The actor playing a major role one night could well be in a minor role the next night (for the repertory system means a rapid change of plays). Further, the Abbey style is based on realism. The speech, gestures, movements and costume are all rooted in local conditions. In contrast to the English and French theatres of the early twentieth century, where 'received pronunciation' and a classical acting style dominated (and were supported by such training centres as RADA, the OUDS, and the Comédie Française), the Abbey Theatre relied on the natural, inherent qualities of the performers. Authenticity took precedence over standardised elocution; the dominant value was 'peasant quality', or truth to native Irish experience.

At the time O'Casey's plays were first performed, an excellent company was in residence at the Abbey. It included the great F. J. McCormick (real name, Peter Judge), Barry Fitzgerald (real name, Will Shields), Sara Allgood, Maureen Delaney, Michael J. Dolan and Gabriel Fallon. The same group of players acted in all of O'Casey's plays written for the Abbey, grew to know his work as intimately as the players at the Moscow Art Theatre knew their Chekhov, and as a result provided performances so convincing that audiences saw them as real. When *Juno* and *The Plough* transferred to London, only some of the original cast were included in the new productions, yet the playing of these original cast-members was recognised in London as startlingly original. The young Laurence Olivier, for example, was bowled over by the performances and vowed one day to play in *Juno*: he directed an outstanding production many years later (1966) at the

National Theatre in London. In short, the Abbey players contributed enormously to the success of the plays on stage.

A final point refers to the staging. The original Abbey Theatre, which was destroyed by fire in 1951, was a small space with a capacity of just over 500 people. The stage was disproportionately small (curtain-line to back wall 16 feet 4 inches, proscenium opening 21 feet, width of stage wall-to-wall 40 feet). These dimensions, coupled with the absence of 'flies' or overhead space, meant that the staging had to be simple. Scenery was functional and unspectacular. Simplicity was the essence of every production. It is important to bear this point in mind because it means – as in the Elizabethan theatre – that a great deal of responsibility was thrown on language to create atmosphere, colour, variety and sheer entertainment. O'Casey's plays were sometimes termed 'Elizabethan' in style (usually by critics in London or New York) and this, basically, is the reason behind it. It is not that O'Casey was trying to be Shakespearean; it is that the theatre conditions required it. (Synge as well as O'Casey virtually wrote poetic prose to compensate for the lack of *mise-en-scène*.) In reading O'Casey's plays, then, it is important not to think the language stilted or artificial but to imagine instead performances where language becomes a major resource which the characters, impoverished though they are, can exploit as a weapon, a defence against deprivation, and a source of rhetorical delight – a kind of richness – even for the poorest of the poor. Thus a new kind of poetry was invented for the modern stage.

References

Greene, David and Edward M. Stephens, *J. M. Synge 1871–1909*, New York: Macmillan, 1959.

O'Casey, Sean, *The Story of the Irish Citizen Army* [1919], in *Feathers from the Green Crow: Sean O'Casey, 1905–1925*, ed. Robert Hogan, Columbia: University of Missouri Press, 1962.

Robinson, Lennox, *The History of the Abbey Theatre 1899–1951*, London: Sidgwick and Jackson, 1951.

Yeats, W. B., 'First Principles (1904)', in *Explorations*, London: Macmillan, 1961.

The Shadow of a Gunman

Introduction

In the opening moments of the BBC/RTE television production of *The Shadow of a Gunman* (1996), the camera pans around the dingy room shared by Davoren and Shields. All is still inside, while outside, in the house and in the street, the ordinary sounds of daily life in a city are heard as people go about their business. The camera picks out a figure buried in bedclothes in a corner of the room: Shields hiding himself away from life (it is 12.30 p.m. though, since curfew is in place, he was in bed early the previous evening). Then the camera settles on the bespectacled figure of Kenneth Branagh as Davoren, seated at a table, staring determinedly into space as he recites a lyric softly. The artist in a garret, we immediately think. A banging on the door and a shouting at Mr Shields have no effect beyond irritating the would-be poet, and thus the day gets under way which is to end in tragedy. It is a wonderful opening, as all plays which begin on a bright, sunny morning usher in hope of new beginnings and great expectations. The cry, 'Are you awake, Mr Shields?' sets the keynote, for this is to be a play about the possibility of two men awakening to moral responsibility.

It is sometimes said that *The Shadow* is an autobiographical play, in which O'Casey himself appears as Donal Davoren. It is true that in 1920, the year in which the play is set, O'Casey roomed with a clerk in Mountjoy

Square, Dublin, and was given 'notice to quit' by the landlord. The roommate, Michael Mullen (1881–1956), later wrote about this short period:

> Life was very unsettled in Dublin at this time, and eighteen visits were made by the police, the English soldiers, the 'Auxies' [Police Auxiliary Cadets] and the Black-and-Tans [British ex-servicemen recruited in 1920 to assist the Royal Irish Constabulary] on the house in which the two of us lived.

The neighbours thought O'Casey was 'on the run' and were kind to him, but he may not have been aware of this. The house was frequented by the outlawed Volunteers and the owner 'was as deep into the movement as anybody in Dublin'. Mullen describes a major raid by the Black-and-Tans in the small hours of one night in March 1921. O'Casey was terrified. He had in his possession the minutes of the Irish Citizen Army (of which he had been secretary in 1914). When daylight came O'Casey smuggled the book out and got rid of it. The raid continued afterwards and there were lots of arrests. As Mullen describes it, the whole incident was terrifying. O'Casey was able to transform it into a tragicomic affair, with a great deal of emphasis on the absurdity of Davoren's position. Also, if Davoren were based solely on O'Casey it would be a devastating form of self-accusation. It is more likely that O'Casey took the details of the experience and imagined the rest: in particular, the situation of the would-be artist whose vanity is a shield for cowardice. In addition, the situation allowed O'Casey to explore the role and responsibility of the artist in times of war, and to dramatise in graphic detail the atmosphere of terror generated by a modern revolutionary struggle.

The basic point, however, is that *The Shadow* was true to working-class conditions in Dublin in the early 1920s. In a recent memoir, the Dublin writer Peter Sheridan describes his first encounter with O'Casey's *The Shadow of a Gunman* when his father began to stage plays in the 1960s:

> From the moment Donal Davoren spoke the opening lines of the play the reality of it engulfed me. It invaded my brain and my heart like nothing had ever done before. Everything about it was genuine Dublin. The words, the dialogue, the situation, the characters. There was no artifice anywhere. This was a community of people caught in a drama, talking to each other, and it unfolded in the most natural and logical way I had ever encountered ... The play was forty years old but a perfect reflection of life. (44: *A Dublin Memoir*, p. 265)

Structure

Nowadays the two-act form is commonplace, but at the time of *The Shadow* it was most unusual. A play was either a one-act or a full-length (i.e., three, four or even five acts). At the time, *The Shadow* could never be a 'stand-alone' presentation but would need a curtain-raiser in one act, as happened when it was premièred on 12 April 1923 (the curtain-raiser was T. C. Murray's *Sovereign Love*). Yet the two-act form suits *The Shadow* admirably. It is an early indication of how unerring O'Casey's dramatic instincts were. One more act would have been superfluous, while to crowd the story into a single act, as some critics still think should have been done, would surely have damaged the symmetrical structure.

We owe the modern preference for the two-act form to

the success and influence of Beckett's *Waiting for Godot* (1953), recently voted the best play of the twentieth century. We may see from *Godot* what the main advantage is: the situation declared in Act One can be repeated or drawn out in Act Two. Of course, Beckett's point is that nothing of significance ever happens; that life is repetition without meaning. O'Casey, who later steadfastly declared he was 'not waiting for Godot', could never see life as absurd in this way. He certainly took a risk, though, in keeping plot to a minimum. The characters in Act One do, indeed, seem rather to be waiting for something to happen than to be interested in taking action themselves (as Tommy Owens ironically testifies). O'Casey deliberately shows us characters who drift in and out of Shields's room, engaging in gossip and self-advertisement, while the only character in Act One who takes action (Maguire) is quickly eliminated. This means that the opening of Act Two, in contrast to the conventional rules of playmaking, does not build on any crisis developed in Act One but instead resumes the conversation between Davoren and Shields which occupied the start of the play. The only factor ticking away in the action since Act One is the bag of bombs left by Maguire. As in the pattern of the 'well-made play' this item must become a vital element in the play's resolution.

The 'well-made play' was a legacy of the nineteenth century. In countless melodramas and murder stories on stage, the dramatic formula first made popular by the French playwrights Eugène Scribe (1791–1861) and Victorien Sardou (1831–1908) was imitated by English writers in the 1890s and after. The formula, in short, was: a situation declared in Act One; a series of crises and complications developed in Act Two, with several 'turning points' registered; and in Act Three an 'obligatory scene' (*scène à faire*), long expected by the audience and often involving an object such as a letter or a fan (as in Oscar Wilde), which is followed by the unravelling (dénouement) of the plot. In such an arrangement all plot details are carefully and mechanically laid down in a cause-and-effect pattern leading inevitably and ingeniously to a dramatic resolution.

Like Shaw, who openly attacked the form of the well-made play, O'Casey usually avoided it and tried instead to reproduce life itself onstage. But his admiration for melo-drama (which was not always as mechanical in operation as the well-made 'mystery' play) drove O'Casey to include some such features in his plays, and Maguire's bag of bombs is an obvious one. We *know* that in due course the bag must be noticed and opened. Further, it is obvious that once the raid begins the bag is incriminating evidence, and it becomes a test of character. Minnie Powell seems at first to resolve the crisis, but this is quickly turned into a tragic development. What cannot be claimed is that the seeds of the final tragedy are apparent from the opening scenes of the play, as would be necessary if the well-made play formula were being followed.

Another example is Mr Gallogher's letter. Although the recitation of the letter is a comic 'turn', a scene existing in its own right as a piece of exaggerated performance, and the characters never reappear in the play, the letter itself becomes dramatically significant in Act Two, just as the raid begins. Davoren suddenly begins to search for the letter, which would be as incriminating as the minute book O'Casey had in his possession in Mullen's room in 1921. Davoren and Shields panic until they find and burn the letter. It does not, in fact, fall into anyone else's hands, as it certainly would in the plot of a well-made play, thus causing complications for other characters. As with the bag of bombs, it is used mainly to expose the characters of Davoren and Shields and to pave the way for the ironic ending.

What these uses and firm control of plot devices show is that for the most part O'Casey made characterisation more important than plot. This emphasis was not new, deriving in fact from naturalism. In the later nineteenth century, particularly in France, writers – novelists first and then serious playwrights – turned away from plot in favour of in-depth characters. As these writers saw it (Zola, Flaubert, Tolstoy, Ibsen, Strindberg, Chekhov, Shaw), the new developments in science made the study of character far more interesting. In particular, the fragmentation of personality in the face of modernity made depiction of the psychological and sociological aspects of character both fascinating and timely. O'Casey, it might be said, followed in the footsteps of the naturalist playwrights when he started writing plays where little seemed to be happening and the structure appeared to offer only a sense of drift rather than of control. It need hardly be said that this sense of drift or casualness in the structure is deceptive. The opening stage-direction refers to 'the might of design' and this is what O'Casey's play, after all, reveals. Things which appear casual and unplanned turn out to have their place in the gradual revelation of a worthless sacrifice, when Minnie dies for Davoren.

Action and Themes

It follows from what has been said about the structure of *The Shadow* that the action is incremental rather than inevitable. Things develop out of haphazard incidents. Even the raid is unexpected and happens for no apparent reason. Yet the play satisfies by and through the details of the plot: the tentative love story, the political conflict, the tragic closure. It is necessary to analyse such details if we are to understand the power of the play to affect us.

O'Casey's original title for the play was *On the Run*. The phrase is a common one in the context of Irish republicanism. It means 'having no home base, keeping on the move in safe houses'. Applied to this play it would be ironic, for Davoren is *not* literally on the run, and this is the whole point. People believe he is and he is happy to let them think so. Yet he himself uses the phrase three times to Shields in Act Two in a non-political sense: he means he intends to leave the dangerous house, to fly. The phrase is a key to the action because it emphasises contingency. There is no stability in the world of the play. Shields, the actual tenant of the room Davoren shares, is given notice to quit by the landlord as the play opens, so he too must soon be on his way. The Black-and-Tans, of course, create instability for all the residents, and actually take Minnie away with them. Thus the action begins to be seen as concerned with unease, impermanence and perpetual motion.

One of the things we notice when first exploring this play is how little relationship there is between the characters. This is not a play about a closely knit family, or a play about the individual's choice between one lover and another, or anything of a kind to engage the feelings of the audience in some basic conflict of interest. What is noteworthy is the *lack* of real engagement among the characters. Davoren and Shields cohabit but seem to have little in common; their lives go in different directions. As we look through the play and observe all the comings and goings, culminating in the raid of the Black-and-Tans, we come to the conclusion that *this* is the action: a series of entrances and exits with no clearly defined or unified purpose. It might be summed up in the writing Davoren does for Minnie: just their two names, without a verb, without even a conjunction. They are juxtaposed in the action; there is not and cannot be any real relationship between them because of Davoren's inauthenticity. He is a pretender, a fake. This juxtaposition, this lack of relational interaction, is borne out when the piece of paper with the two names on it is found on Minnie's body after she is shot. Her blood has run over the paper, erasing Davoren's name. Nothing survives to link her with him. His identity is blotted out. The action, then, might be described as a series of juxtapositions, of failed attempts to relate. There is no direct relationship, for example, between Mr Gallogher, Mrs Henderson and what happens to Minnie: yet Minnie's presence during the reading of Gallogher's letter strengthens her belief that Davoren really *is* an important terrorist and so *indirectly* Gallogher's letter motivates her to carry through her plan to save Davoren. But all actions in the play are indirect in that way.

The result is that, added together, these actions which pile up within the play in lieu of a plot create a massive irony. Minnie's death is ironic. Her motive is to save a man she thinks is a republican hero but she dies in vain for a coward. The circumstances of Minnie's death – she jumps from the British Army lorry when the IRA ambush the Black-and-Tans – are also ironic, for she is shot in the bosom when she jumps down. It is likely that she is shot by her own side, so to speak, the IRA.

Once we have registered this, the major irony of the play, we are in a position to observe how thematic irony runs throughout *The Shadow of a Gunman*. It is ironic that Mr Gallogher's letter in fact calls for IRA intervention in the tenements and that they actually arrive to ambush the 'Tans and kill Minnie. This is a complete coincidence but it underlines the major point O'Casey is making: in a guerilla-war situation anything can happen, for there is no order, no foreseeable pattern. The 'might of design' falls apart and accident or contingency prevails. This theme is comically voiced by Mr Grigson: 'You're sure of your life nowhere now; it's just as safe to go everywhere as it is to [go] anywhere' (p. 49). This theme is expanded by Shields: 'It's the civilians that suffer; when there's an ambush they don't know where to run. Shot in the back to save the British Empire, an' shot in the breast to save the soul of Ireland' (pp. 39–40). This is the major truth of the play. It turns out – ironically – to be Minnie's fate exactly.

A related theme to the contingency factor during urban guerilla warfare is the theme of sacrifice and victimisation. Shields, a major spokesman against the violence, sees that the romantic features of a war of independence have now rapidly disappeared in Ireland, to be replaced by a harsher reality. Within that reality, it is impossible to regard Ireland as a Yeatsian 'Cathleen Ni Houlihan', that is as a romantic goddess for whom young men will willingly sacrifice themselves. Yeats's one-act play *Cathleen Ni Houlihan* (1902), with his lover Maud Gonne playing the leading role, had given new life to the old myth of Ireland as a pathetic woman deprived of her possessions but renewed in hope and youth through the blood-sacrifice of patriots. By the year 1920, with terrorism rampant and reprisals a weekly occurrence, the shine had gone from Yeats's romantic image. O'Casey demythologises the blood-sacrifice by dwelling on the ordinary civilians who are innocently swept into a violence which goes in all directions. Shields dismisses Cathleen Ni Houlihan, 'for she's a ragin' divil now, an' if you only look crooked at her you're sure of a punch in th' eye' (p. 39). Because he is frightened by this change, Shields can see no value in any sacrifice now; Maguire's death leaves him cold. Minnie he dismisses as a feather-headed and dangerous threat to respectability: 'I wouldn't care to have me life dependin' on brave little Minnie Powell – she wouldn't sacrifice a jazz dance to save it' (p. 38). Again, the irony of this prediction is all too clear. Minnie's sacrifice, romantic in motivation, is genuine. Her action exposes Shields's own short-sightedness and cynicism, as well as his and Davoren's cowardice. Thus O'Casey balances the anti-sacrifice emphasis in the play with Minnie's genuine if totally misdirected martyrdom. For any tragedy, of course, there must be a sacrificial victim.

Another major theme in the play is 'shadow and substance'. It is not quite the same as the appearance-versus-reality theme found in a lot of comedy, from *The Merchant of Venice* ('all that glisters is not gold') to Shaw's *Candida* (where the weak Marchbanks turns out stronger than the manly Morell) and Wilde's *The Importance of Being Earnest* (where nothing is as it seems). It is closer to the use of the theme in Synge's *The Playboy of the Western World* (1907). In Synge's play, Christy Mahon is in reality a timid, lonely young man oppressed by his dominating father. But when he tells the community he runs to that he has killed his father they worship him as a hero; from that moment he is reconstructed and given a sense of identity based on the imagination of the people. Christy is transformed. Even though it turns out that his father is not dead and returns to punish him, Christy has *become* a hero in the course of the action. Largely, this happens through the love of Pegeen Mike and the confidence her admiration gives him. In the end it does not matter that he told a lie and had not, in fact, killed his father (though he had tried/intended to): what matters is that Christy has been liberated by his reception, for the people are 'after making a mighty man of me this day by the power of a lie'. The enabling power of myth-making is here revealed. In O'Casey's play Davoren, like Christy Mahon, allows a lie to grow around his identity, and feeds off Minnie's admiration. She and the other residents build up Davoren as a kind of 'playboy' in Synge's sense. Unlike Christy Mahon, Davoren knows well that he is playing false. But he thinks at the end of Act One, 'what danger can there be in being the shadow of a gunman?' (p. 32).

The difference between O'Casey's treatment of the theme and Synge's, however, is that Davoren does not change. There is no transformation. Shadow does not become substance as happens in *The Playboy*, where Christy goes away joyously at the end, victorious over his father and determined to 'go romancing through a romping lifetime from this hour to the dawning of the judgment day'. On the contrary, Davoren ends up more shadowy than ever, his stature reduced by his failure to rise to the level Minnie Powell foolishly placed him at. After all, where Synge was writing comedy, O'Casey was writing tragedy.

Characters

Some account has already been given above of the main characters in *The Shadow of a Gunman*, but it may be useful to focus more directly on their features here. The first point we should note is that O'Casey makes the setting a factor in the characterisation. This is in line with naturalistic theory, based on Darwin's emphasis on the deterministic influence of environment and heredity. Thus Seumas Shields inhabits a world of *'absolute untidiness'*, the result of *'congenital slovenliness'* (p. 3). O'Casey describes Shields as 'primitive', by which he means subjected to irrational fears of the supernatural: *'In him is frequently manifested the superstition, the fear and the malignity of primitive man'* (p. 4). Shields is a comic foil to Davoren; he is quickly revealed as ultra-Catholic and religious (he goes to daily Mass) and yet refuses to pay his rent and counts the bundles of spoons in case there might be *more* than a dozen in them. He is also superstitious to the point of absurdity. He believes in ghosts and sees significance in the 'tappin' on the wall' in Act Two (p. 36); in the end he is convinced that the tragedy was the result of this supernatural tapping. Shields's hypocrisy is revealed in his rejoicing over Shelley's possible confinement in hell (the poet Percy Bysshe Shelley took a special interest in Irish affairs and visited Dublin in 1812 to urge the people to further rebellion). In addition, Shields is a coward. When the Black-and-Tans arrive he panics. He makes sure to give the English version of his name, Jimmie, in case the Gaelic version might suggest republican sympathies. He is terrified when the Auxiliary pokes a gun under his nose. He is equally terrified that Minnie Powell will betray him (and Davoren). He is thus revealed as entirely self-centred, hypocritical and pusillanimous; yet he is a comic figure. He is assertive with the landlord when he clearly has no case; he is a hopeless salesman, as Mrs Henderson testifies (the children mock him with the nickname 'oul' hairpins', p. 29), and talks too much to be efficient; he has a store of literary information – he can identify quotations in a surprising way – which suggests the self-taught (we are reminded of Alexander Pope's line, 'A little learning is a dangerous thing'); and once a moment of danger has passed, Shields reconstructs it ludicrously to his own advantage. This last point reveals Shields at his most unconsciously entertaining. Terrified though he plainly is when the Auxiliary swaggers around the room brandishing a gun, Shields has to supply a totally different version when Grigson enters with his invented tale of heroic indifference. When the noise of bombs and gunfire interrupts this made-up story, Shields hides himself and then refuses to accept that Minnie Powell's death has anything to do with him. The rapid transition from boaster to coward is comic.

On the positive side, Shields offers some telling comments on the changes in the Irish political scene. His experience as an enthusiast for Gaelic culture and as a nationalist lends force to his comments. We accept him as a credible witness to the violence and the chaos which reign outside. The fact that Shields has dropped out of the 'movement' is meant to suggest his inability to cope with the realities of revolution as distinct from romantic cultural offshoots. All in all, Shields is a clearly drawn representation of an Irish lower-middle-class type, half committed to faith and fatherland but more committed to self-preservation and self-love. He stands condemned for his cowardice. The question posed at the start, 'Are you awake, Mr Shields?' can finally be answered in the negative. Shields, unlike Davoren, never awakens to the reality of his own self-absorption.

Donal Davoren may well in part be an ironic self-portrait of Sean O'Casey, as suggested already, but if so it is a remarkably honest one. Is O'Casey accusing himself of cowardice for failing to commit himself to the Irish revolution? Is he exorcising in this play feelings of guilt for allowing others to sacrifice themselves on his behalf for national independence? There may well be such forces at work in this 'portrait of the artist', and yet so merciless is the exposure that one must also believe that O'Casey is rather tracing *consequences of a position taken* than deliberately mocking his own situation. No doubt it helped O'Casey that he, like Davoren, was a minor poet who, in 1918, published some popular, sentimental love poetry. But then in later years O'Casey said Davoren was a consumptive insurance agent he knew.

In any case, O'Casey also shared Shields's experience. Having been a member of the Irish Republican Brotherhood and having learned Irish (Gaelic) so that he could speak and write it fluently, O'Casey was certainly, before socialism claimed him, 'as good a Gael as some that are knocking about now' (p. 9). In short, there are parts of O'Casey in Shields as well as in Davoren; for the matter of that, there are parts of O'Casey in Mr Grigson, since O'Casey was a staunch Protestant in his earlier years, and mingled with Orangemen in his parish of St Barnabas in Dublin's East Wall area. All this tells us is that the dramatist commonly draws on different areas in his own experience in order to create a variety of characters. Davoren is thus not really a self-portrait but a creation within a dramatic design which goes well beyond

O'Casey's actual experience. If one turns to his auto-biography, one finds in Book 4 (*Inishfallen, Fare Thee Well*), a chapter entitled 'The Raid' which gives quite a different outcome from either the account given by his roommate Michael Mullen or that dramatised in *The Shadow*. 'The Raid' invents a romantic encounter with a married woman, which is farcically interrupted by the arrival of the Black-and-Tans. The play, likewise, is invention, modifying and expanding details from O'Casey's life and shaping these to form a tragic outcome.

Davoren, like Shields, is first defined (in the opening stage-direction) against his environment, an untidy room incapable of 'improvement'. He is described as seriously divided psychologically, between '*a desire for activity*' and '*an unquenchable tendency towards rest*'. His struggles through life, strangely enough, 'have been handicapped' by an inherent belief in the importance of art (pp. 3–4). Here O'Casey quotes from Shaw's *The Doctor's Dilemma* (1906), Act Four, where the artist Louis Dubedat states his belief not in God or divine redemption but 'in the might of design, the mystery of colour, the redemption of all things by Beauty everlasting'. Davoren quotes the first phrase in Act Two when he denies that the poet's role is to save the people (p. 35). This is the source of Davoren's conflict and confusion. He wants to be an artist of the kind he mistakenly imagines Shelley to have been, wrapped up in himself and the meditation of beauty. He wants to ignore life around him and to concentrate on his writing. But life keeps bursting in on him; he can get no privacy and determines to go 'on the run' out of this room, *not*, as the phrase suggests, to continue service to a freedom movement but to hide himself in a romantic notion of the artist as a solitary. The play shows how selfish, vain and destructive such an aim can be. O'Casey allows Shields to point out that 'a poet's claim to greatness depends upon his power to put passion in the common people' (p. 35). How could Davoren ever do this if he himself has no passion for social justice? So, Davoren is handicapped not so much, as the opening stage-direction declares, by a belief in the importance of art as by a *mistaken* belief in its function. Art is a social construct; it demands an audience and it interacts with that audience. It may, of course, attempt to be elitist and ignore the ordinary people. Strangely enough, the foolish Shields is able to put his finger on it: 'it doesn't pay a working-man to write poetry' (p. 35). Because Davoren aspires to elitism and yet lives among the common people he is confused and not wholly a person at all. He is bloated with a sense of his own importance.

Davoren's vanity is obvious. He talks loftily about poetry and art and is easily flattered by those in awe of him for quite other (mistaken) reasons. His hunger for recognition as an artist is satisfied by the recognition of himself as a gunman. His acceptance of Mr Gallogher's letter is a major confession of that vanity. He cannot bear to refuse because to do so would lose him some, however misguided, admiration. He thrives on the respect shown him by characters as different as Mrs Henderson and Mr Grigson. Above all he thrives on the infatuation shown by Minnie Powell, and here he is irresponsible. His vanity causes him to deceive her shamefully. If the play were longer the plot would doubtless involve a seduction and betrayal as happens in *Juno and the Paycock*. As it is, time does not allow what is clearly implied. It could be said that Davoren's vanity causes Minnie's death.

Equally, Davoren's cowardice causes her death. For,

like Shields, Davoren is at bottom a coward. This becomes obvious in his panic over the letter and the bag of bombs. When the raid begins, Davoren, incapable of taking action to hide the bombs, *'reclines almost fainting on the bed'* (p. 52), and has to rely on Minnie's cool head to extricate him from this mortal danger. He is a complete *anti*-hero.

Although Davoren, unlike Shields, comes to see his guilt and feels shame for Minnie's death, it has to be asked whether, in fact, he actually changes. The experience of humiliation is profound: he recognises himself as 'poet and poltroon' (coward), but he still continues to make pretty phrases about himself and his woe. He still quotes Shelley as he did at the beginning, 'Ah me, alas! Pain, pain, pain ever, for ever!' (p. 62). If ever there was a time for him to drop the fancy talk and speak in simple words of grief this is it. But he bursts into self-pity, addressing himself in the third person: 'Oh, Donal Davoren, shame is your portion now,' and continues with a quotation from the Bible (Ecclesiastes 12: 6). Davoren stands exposed as a self-centred individual, doomed never to be more than the shadow of a human being.

Minnie Powell, in total contrast, is a delightful creation. Once again, it is important when reading O'Casey's plays to pay close attention to his stage-directions. She is described as having *'a force and an assurance beyond her years'* (twenty-three). Left an orphan, she developed qualities of independence and courage. It is plain that we are meant to admire her and empathise with her *'easy confidence'* even in the company of *'those of a superior education'* (p. 14) such as Davoren. She is lively, charming and yet, unfortunately, naïve. She would have made a good wife for Davoren because she would have forced him to abandon his stuffy habit of using quotations or classical allusion and to speak and behave like an ordinary human being. For example, we have the early exchange when she tells Davoren about Tommy Owens:

MINNIE: ... (*ecstatically*) he's a gorgeous melodeon player!
DAVOREN: A gifted son of Orpheus, eh?
MINNIE: (*who never heard of Orpheus*) You've said it, Mr Davoren: the son of poor oul' Battie Owens, a weeshy, dawny, bit of a man that was never sober an' was always talkin' politics ... (p. 15)

She comes out of this exchange higher in our estimation than Davoren. And so it is when she asks about his poetry. She is a romantic and he, replying to her remarks on Robert Burns and Annie Laurie, patronises her with his sophisticated debunking of her views on self-sacrifice. Yet in this opening conversation between them Minnie displays her independence. She will not be pressured into taking notice of what people might say about her visiting Davoren (something several characters comment on: Mrs Henderson, Shields, Mrs Grigson). Davoren recognises Minnie's unusual quality, this reckless indifference to the opinions of society around her. He calls her his 'soul within' (p. 19), his other self; and yet he is about to destroy that soul, and in so doing destroy himself. Minnie is vulnerable through her undisguised infatuation, and her wholeheartedness makes her attractive. She is foolish, no doubt, but O'Casey's representation of woman here contrasts quite sharply with his portrait of Mrs Grigson in Act Two: Mrs Grigson is so completely dominated by her husband as to be virtually his slave. Minnie Powell would never be any man's slave. Being fearless, she will choose the man she wants and will thereafter protect and care for him, just as she would expect him to protect and care for her. Impulsive as she is, it is natural for her to burst into the room in Act Two and volunteer to take away any incriminating evidence. This generous gesture costs her her life. In effect, she trusts too far in the chivalry of men; she thought she would not be hurt because she was a woman. And indeed she would have been safe enough had she been content to shelter in the army lorry and had not taken sides by shouting 'Up the Republic!' (p. 58) and jumping down into the street. Her bravery was foolish; and yet naïve and romantic though Minnie is politically, she emerges as vastly superior in moral terms to the man she misread, Donal Davoren.

Language

O'Casey's language is both realistic and poetic. Although this is a paradox it is probably the key to understanding O'Casey's procedures. On the one hand the Abbey tradition was predominantly realistic, using onstage the speech of the Irish people in all its regional and dialectical forms. A glance at P. W. Joyce's *English As We Speak It in Ireland* (1910) indicates what this means. English spoken in Ireland is historically inflected: as the language of the coloniser it retained a lot of words, phrases and pronunciation dating from the sixteenth to the eighteenth centuries. For example, the word 'bedlam' is used by the 'Voice at the Door' trying to awaken Shields: 'Why don't you get up, then, an' not have the house turned into a bedlam tryin' to waken you?' (p. 4). (The word retains its sixteenth-century reference to Bethlehem madhouse in

London.) And the epithet 'dawny', which Minnie applies to Tommy Owens's father (p. 15), is the seventeenth-century English word 'donny', meaning 'weak, in poor health'. Such words, however, surface only occasionally; far more common are Hiberno-English usages based on Gaelic usages. For centuries Ireland was bilingual, and when in the nineteenth century English gradually displaced Gaelic, the language spoken (and, in certain instances, written) incorporated words and grammatical constructions borrowed from Gaelic. By the 1920s many Gaelic words had been widely assimilated, even into urban speech. Thus in *The Shadow* we encounter 'gosthering', 'mallavoging', 'traneen' and 'whisht'. In addition, spoken English continued to include Gaelic constructions, such as Minnie's 'Do you be all alone all the day, Mr Davoren?' (p. 15). This is based on the Gaelic form of the continuous present tense; in standard English the sentence would run, 'Are you alone all the day?' Other constructions taken from Gaelic include the use of conjunction with present participle to express 'while' ('an' we sittin' at the table', p. 43), and the use of a compound with 'after' to express the perfect tense ('after takin' his tea', p. 43). The phrase 'it's meself that hopes you're feelin' well', addressed by the landlord to Shields (p. 10), is another example of Gaelic usage absorbed by Dublin speech. Syntax in Gaelic is more flexible than in standard English, and allows word-order to be dictated by whatever requires emhasis. Thus Shields, referring to Maguire's unfortunate death, says: 'two of them he got, one through each lung' (p. 34). It would make a worthwhile exercise to go through the play and select the usages which strike the reader as Hiberno-English, as these are part of the richness and energy of O'Casey's language. P. S. O'Hegarty, one of the early critics of *The Shadow*, said (O'Hegarty, p. 53): 'It is a gramophone record of the Dublin accent.'

There is a strange tension in the language used in *The Shadow*, between realism and poetic, or heightened, speech. O'Casey seems, on one level, to be recording ordinary speech, even to the point of spelling phonetically (for example, 'me' for 'my', 'be' for 'by' and 'av' for 'of' in Grigson's northern dialect). But there is less phonetic spelling than in *Juno* or *The Plough*. In those plays, O'Casey was trying for pure realism; here, although the dialogue is natural, it is also highly elaborated – if not as obviously heightened as in J. M. Synge's plays – to provide a kind of poetry in prose. All of the characters, with the exception of Minnie and Maguire, use language rhetorically. It is a resource for them in their poverty. Raymond Williams insisted that O'Casey's language is a *form* of poverty, evidence 'of a starved, showing-off imagination'. To most observers, however, the indulgence in rhetoric is a kind of richness, as of a people who have perfected the 'gift of the gab'. (It is difficult to comment on this richness without beginning to patronise.) O'Casey accords these characters a poetic facility, a control over alliteration, repetition, hyperbole, and, above all, rhythm.

In a sense, the play as a whole is about language. It opens with the poet Davoren reciting his own (rather bad) verse and in the first few pages of text the emphasis is on words and their possible meanings. References to Morpheus, god of sleep, associated with the poppy, symbol of sacrifice in the 1914–18 war, lead on to Prometheus, the god who brought fire to humanity, and then to *Prometheus Unbound*, a poetic drama written by Shelley. A chain of associations is being forged, making myth impinge on the tenements; it leads to the underworld, which Orpheus visited, or 'hell', which is mentioned several times. The setting itself is thus established as a form of hell from which liberation must be found; an obvious link is Shields's description of Minnie as 'a Helen of Troy come to live in a tenement!' (p. 37). The contrast is meant to be ironic; Minnie is no goddess, and yet the mythic reference effectively shows how unheroic is the male world she inhabits.

When Mr Gallogher arrives with his letter we enjoy a comic interlude. But we should also be aware of the concentration in the whole scene on rhetoric, language, the right word. Davoren is placed in the position of critic and literary mentor; he is clearly embarrassed by Gallogher's ridiculous style, but we can see that Davoren's own literary efforts are hardly much better. Mrs Henderson's criticism of the letter is probably just as astute as Davoren's and it is at least positive: she suggests the addition of the word 'shocking' as an improvement. Everybody in the scene becomes involved in the question of style. Mrs Henderson sets the tone with her 'there's a beginnin' for you, Mr Davoren' (p. 25), which is immediately echoed by Minnie ('That's some swank') and even by Tommy Owens (no literary critic at the best of times, though he does venture the view that 'shocking' is spelt with two 'k's). Gallogher's letter is a pedantic exercise, full of strange, legalistic terms and unnecessary definitions, but its approval ('It's the most powerfullest letter I ever heard read', p. 28) shows how much rhetoric means to these people. Their regard for language, their delight in a well-articulated sentence, is proof that they are rich in appreciation of literacy if deprived of material wealth. All of this proves how blind Davoren is when he asserts that the people 'live in the abyss, [while] the poet lives on the mountain-top', and that to the people 'beauty is for sale in a butcher's shop' (p. 35). He fails to see that the difference between him and them is only one of degree. And because of this failure he will always fail to communicate and will use poetry as a means of escape from the world around him.

Therefore, there is within the play itself a justification for the characters' use of a poeticised, rather literary mode of speech. For example, when Shields describes how Ireland has become more violent, he lapses into a Joycean style of parodying the Apostles' Creed: 'I believe in the gun almighty, maker of heaven an' earth' (p. 39), a sentence concluding a whole speech which cleverly makes a play between the words 'prayer' and 'warfare' ('Instead of counting their beads now they're countin' bullets; their Hail Marys and paternosters [Our Fathers] are burstin' bombs ... '). Adolphus Grigson, too, glories in the sound of his own voice, likes to use a string of rhetorical questions, to quote the Bible and deliver a 'dangerous' (anti-Catholic) song, 'The Orange Lily O' (pp. 47–8). With Grigson we find an equation between language and drink: indulgence in one is as intoxicating as indulgence in the other. The justification is thus ironic, for all this lively use of language for the most part leads nowhere, and this is O'Casey's point. It is all so much hot air, glorified pub-talk like Tommy Owens's self-dramatisation under the influence. The only really genuine expression possible within the play is Minnie Powell's 'Up the Republic!' heard offstage (p. 58). And the point about this cry is that it is falsified by Minnie's delusion that she is serving Davoren's cause. The justification always rings hollow, and we should read the play with an awareness of both its linguistic richness and the hollowness of that language. There is, as has been remarked by Bernice Schrank, a constant pattern in the play of words disassociated from deeds.

The Play in Performance

The Abbey Theatre first staged *The Shadow of a Gunman* for only three nights from Thursday to Saturday, 12–14 April 1923. This marked the end of the season, and it is likely O'Casey's play was given this slot because the directors were unsure how it might fare: if it flopped, then little harm could be done to the Abbey. But in fact the new play made a growing impact, with an excellent cast, including Arthur Shields as Donal Davoren, F. J. McCormick as Seumas Shields and Michael J. Dolan as Tommy Owens. The play was directed by Lennox Robinson, the playwright and manager.

One reason why the Abbey was cautious about O'Casey's play was that the civil war was still raging (until the end of April 1923) and the theatre was under armed guard from 25 March 1923 because of threatened reprisals by the IRA following the Abbey's public acceptance of the Anglo-Irish Treaty. The Abbey had been the only Dublin theatre which had not closed when ordered to by the IRA as a gesture against the Treaty. Since Yeats was now a Senator in the new Free State government, the Abbey was doubly vulnerable to terrorist attack. It was thought prudent to enter a warning in the theatre programme that the sounds in Act Two of a lorry and gunfire were part of the play's action. (There was a bomb scare in a neighbouring cinema on the Friday night.) It is not surprising that the audience on opening night was rather meagre. But on succeeding nights, when word of mouth promoted the originality of *The Shadow*, attendance shot up and a 'house full' notice was displayed on the final night – the first for years at the Abbey, then on the verge of bankruptcy. In her *Journals*, Lady Gregory said that the last night's audience was the largest at the Abbey since the première of Shaw's *The Shewing Up of Blanco Posnet* in 1909 – and that had been a special case, since that controversial play attracted international theatre critics primed for more riots. Lady Gregory brought O'Casey outside to see the crowd queuing: 'Many, to my grief, had to be turned away from the door.' Art and reality certainly intermingled during the first production of this play – amusingly, the armed guard came inside to instruct the actor playing the Auxiliary how to hold his revolver.

The critical response was based on two things: how well the play captured the realities of the war of independence, and how amusingly satirical the character portraits were. One reviewer mentioned the audience 'squirming with laughter and revelling boisterously in the satire'. Probably because of the need for relief inside the theatre from the grim realities of what threatened outside, critics and audiences preferred to ignore the tragic side of O'Casey's play. The reviewer for the prestigious *Irish Times* even urged O'Casey to 'remove the small element of real tragedy from the end of his play' and call it a satire instead (Hogan, p. 146).

The Shadow of a Gunman returned to the Abbey stage when it reopened for one of the major social events of the year, Horse Show Week, on 6 August 1923, after which it became firmly established in the repertory. By this time the civil war was over and Dublin was at peace. Lennox Robinson, the director, was surprised to find that in 1924 *The Shadow* continued to be popular:

I thought that much of its success might be due to the fact that the author was giving expression to the audience's feelings with regard to our civil war ... But in days of peace the play has the same success ... which I must attribute to its veracity ... [But] I am curious to see it play before an audience which will not recognise it for the pitiless photograph it is, curious to see how it will stand that test.

That test came in London (in the Court Theatre) on 27 May 1927, where it ran for sixty-four performances. Directed by Arthur Sinclair, a player from the early days of the Abbey who now played Seumas Shields, the cast included Synge's lover Molly Allgood (as Mrs Grigson), her sister Sara Allgood (as Mrs Henderson), Sydney Morgan (as Adolphus Grigson) and Harry Hutchinson as Donal Davoren. A newcomer, Eileen Carey, played Minnie Powell. (O'Casey admired her enormously; they became lovers and married in London on 23 September.) The London première of *The Shadow* came after the London premières of both *Juno and the Paycock* (November 1925) and *The Plough and the Stars* (May 1926). Audiences therefore knew what to expect, and reviewers tended to see *The Shadow* in the light of these two greater achievements. The same can be said of the Abbey Players' touring production in New York in October 1932; the play had had its American première at the Goodman Theatre in Chicago in April 1929, which was not a success.

What the London reviews of 1927 indicate is that Dublin was not alone in finding *The Shadow* rather too hilarious. One reviewer remarked that although the play read like a tragedy it was played 'like a farce'. This mixture of comedy and tragedy was perceived as 'very Irish'. Nevertheless, the more astute critics found the constant laughter of the audience an irritation, although the playwright was also blamed for structuring the play so that the comedy overshadowed the tragedy. A lot of the blame derived from the focus on Seumas Shields rather than Davoren. The balance of the play is easily upset if this is allowed to happen in performance.

There were no fewer than thirty-six productions of *The Shadow* at the Abbey before O'Casey introduced a ban in 1958 on the professional production of his plays in Ireland. (The ban resulted from clerical opposition to O'Casey's *The Drums of Father Ned*, written for the Dublin Theatre Festival in 1958. Furious over what he saw as censorship both of his play and of an adaptation of Joyce's *Ulysses* intended for the programme, O'Casey withdrew *Father Ned* amid loud controversy, the Theatre Festival was cancelled for that year, and O'Casey refused permission for the professional production of any of his plays in Ireland.) He lifted that ban by special request in 1964 and there have been eight further productions at the Abbey to date. Meanwhile, there have been notable revivals in England. Jack McGowran directed *The Shadow* at the Mermaid in April 1967, and Michael Bogdanov directed the RSC's production at Stratford in March 1980 (to mark the centenary of O'Casey's birth). Whereas McGowran (who played Seumas Shields) seems to have repeated Arthur Sinclair's error of overemphasising the comedy, Bogdanov, by casting Michael Pennington (an actor acclaimed for his Hamlet) as Donal Davoren opposite Norman Rodway's Shields, got results found to be both 'exhilarating' and a successful balance between the serious and comic elements in the play. This success was achieved in spite of the difficulties in staging this play, carefully written for a proscenium stage, in the arena-style space offered by the Other Place. This shows clearly that with intelligent direction and a proper balance in the casting, O'Casey's *The Shadow* can triumph on the modern stage. The TV production cited at the outset, with Kenneth Branagh as Davoren and Stephen Rea as Shields, admirably achieved this necessary balance.

Textual Notes

4 bedlam – madhouse.

5 Angelus – bell calling to prayer at 12 noon and 6 p.m.

– land of Saints and Scholars – title given to Ireland in the Middle Ages.

6 Kathleen Ni Houlihan – allegorical name for Ireland, much used by the poets.

– Shelley – Percy Bysshe Shelley (1792–1822), romantic poet and radical. Among his early writings were two pamphlets, *The Necessity of Atheism* (1811) and *An Address to the Irish People* (1812). His long dramatic poem *Prometheus Unbound* was written in 1819.

7 Cuchullian – properly 'Cuchulain', the Celtic hero.

– Black-and-Tans – British ex-servicemen recruited and sent to Ireland in 1920 to help the demoralised Royal Irish Constabulary suppress the Irish revolutionaries. Detested by the majority of the Irish, their nickname derived from their black tunics and khaki trousers.

9 Irish Republican Brotherhood (IRB) – a secret organisation, founded in America in the mid-nineteenth century, dedicated to Irish nationalism.

O'Casey became a member in Dublin, *c.* 1906, but abandoned republicanism for socialism in 1913.

- Balor of the Evil Eye – in Celtic mythology, the god of death, whose one eye destroyed the onlooker.

- James Stephens – (1825–1901); not the writer, but the republican revolutionary, founder of the IRB in 1858.

10 gostherin' – gossiping (Hiberno-English).

11 green, white and yellow – the colours of the Irish flag.

13 Banba – Ireland.

14 Oh, proud were the chieftains – lines by Thomas Davis (1814–45).

15 Orpheus – in Greek mythology, a musician capable of making trees dance, wild beasts tame, etc.

16 the men o' '98 – the United Irishmen who fought to break the link with England in 1798 (and lost).

- One day when Morn's – these lines, like most of the poetry Davoren recites (apart from Shelley) is O'Casey's own.

18 Bobbie Burns – Robert Burns (1756–96), Scotland's national poet.

19–20 'grasp this sorry scheme of things entire' – a quotation from the *Rubáiyát of Omar Khayyám* (1859), translated by Edward Fitzgerald.

21 'High upon the gallows tree' – a patriotic poem about the so-called Manchester Martyrs (Fenians), published 1867.

22 Sarsfield – Patrick Sarsfield (d. 1693), Irish patriot who fought against the forces of King William of Orange. Tommy Owens foolishly places him in 1798.

- Vinegar Hill – in County Wexford, site of a famous battle in 1798.

25 decomposed – composed, an example of Mrs Henderson's not infrequent malapropisms.

26 Republican Courts . . . foreign Courts – after the massive Sinn Féin victory in the 1918 general election, a provisional government was established in Dublin and native republican courts set up.

28 Sinn Féin Amhain – (Gaelic) Ourselves Alone.

29 mallavogin' – beating, chastisement (from the Gaelic).

 – whisht – quiet!

33 'The cold chaste moon . . .' – from Shelley's poem 'Epipsychidion' (1821).

34 digs – lodgings, or 'diggings', a term used in World War I for trenches.

38 a British Tommy with a Mons Star – an English soldier decorated for serving in France in 1914. In republican circles to marry a British soldier is to betray the cause.

34 De Profundis is 'The Soldiers' Song' – instead of Psalm 130 they sing what was to become Ireland's national anthem, written by Peadar Kearney (1883–1942), uncle to Brendan Behan.

43 too far gone in the horns – too old (to change).

45 mindin' you – taking notice of you.

46 goughers – louts (Dublin dialect, see Dolan, *Dictionary of Hiberno-English*).

47 Orangeman – member of the Orange Order, founded in Northern Ireland in 1794 in a sectarian move against Catholic workers in the linen industry and organised along the lines of the Freemasons. There were Orangemen in O'Casey's parish of St Barnabas, in the East Wall area of Dublin.

 – Tone, Emmet an' Parnell – three Irish patriots:

Theobald Wolfe Tone (1763–98), Robert Emmet (1778–1803) and Charles Stewart Parnell (1846–91). The latter was the advocate of Home Rule detested by Orangemen like Grigson.

- King William ... battle av the Boyne – here Grigson recites a rival historical record to the republican. King William was the great Protestant defender, whose victory over King James II at the Boyne in 1690 was a landmark in Irish history.

51 Mills bombs – grenades.

53 Tommies ... Tans – Tommies, or British soldiers, could be expected to be more civilised than the 'Tans'.

- Auxiliaries – Police Auxiliary Cadets, or 'Auxies', recruited from ex-British officers to assist the Royal Irish Constabulary in Ireland.

55 ikey – clever, experienced.

56 Mr Moody an' Mr Sankey – Dwight Lyman Moody (1837–91) and Ira D. Sankey (1840–1908) were two American evangelists who toured Britain in 1873 and 1883.

- the silver cord is loosened ... broken – a quotation from the Bible, Ecclesiastes 12: 6.

62 poltroon – coward.

References

Gregory, Lady, *Journals 1916–1930*, ed. Lennox Robinson, London: Putman, 1946, pp. 71–3.

Hogan, Robert and Richard Burnham, *The Years of O'Casey 1921–1926*, Modern Irish Drama, vol. vi, Gerrards Cross: Colin Smythe, 1992.

Joyce, P. W., *English As We Speak It in Ireland*, with

introduction by Terence Dolan, Dublin: Wolfhound
Press, 1988.

O'Casey, Sean, 'The Raid', in *Inishfallen, Fare Thee Well*,
London: Pan Books, 1972, pp. 48–63.

– 'Not Waiting for Godot', in *Blasts and Benedictions*,
ed. Ronald Ayling, London: Macmillan, 1967, pp. 51–2.

O'Hegarty, P. S., 'A Drama of Disillusionment (1924)', in
The Dublin Trilogy: A Casebook, ed. Ronald Ayling,
London: Macmillan, 1985, pp. 52–3.

Shaw, George Bernard, *The Doctor's Dilemma*, in
Complete Plays, 6 vols., New York: Dodd, Mead, 1,
p. 173.

Schrank, Bernice, ' "You needn't say no more": Language
and the Problem of Communication in Sean O'Casey's
The Shadow of a Gunman', in *The Dublin Trilogy: A
Casebook*, ed. Ronald Ayling, London: Macmillan,
1985, pp. 67–80.

Sheridan, Peter, *44: A Dublin Memoir*, London:
Macmillan, 1999, pp. 262–73.

Synge, J. M., *The Playboy of the Western World*, in
Complete Plays, ed. Ann Saddlesmyer, Oxford: Oxford
University Press, 1995.

Williams, Raymond, *Drama from Ibsen to Brecht*,
Harmondsworth: Penguin, 1976, pp. 161–9.

Juno and the Paycock

Introduction

When *Juno and the Paycock* was first staged at the Abbey Theatre in March 1924 it was an immediate smash hit. This was something new. The Abbey had been in dire financial trouble and was on the verge of bankruptcy. Indeed, after O'Casey's *The Shadow of a Gunman* was staged in 1923 it was made known to O'Casey that it might be better if he could wait to be paid until the bank was able to pass the cheque. O'Casey courteously agreed, and eventually got a cheque for less than five pounds, a huge disappointment. But that play began the upturn in the theatre's fortunes. Each time it was revived in repertory it packed out, bringing a new, broadly based audience into the Abbey. This audience now turned up in large numbers night after night to see *Juno*, which they recognised as a play not only hilarious but truthful, not only peopled with characters instantly recognisable as Dubliners but also descriptive of the very tense, threatening and violent conditions they had just gone through in the civil war (1922–3). The immediacy of the play, the excellence of the acting, and the combination of comedy and tragedy so successfully achieved, contributed to this unprecedented success. Soon the Abbey was out of financial trouble.

To some, the attraction of *Juno* could be explained by its 'photographic' realism. One critic, for example, commented: 'O'Casey is a photographic artist who retouches his films with an acid pencil to produce an effect of grotesque satire' (Malone, p. 68). This is something O'Casey always denied. He disliked mere realism, drama as a 'slice of life'; for him drama had to include a lot more colour, melodrama and popular entertainment than Ibsenist realism would ever allow. The power of *Juno* resides more in its inclusiveness than in its concentration on unity of theme or action. In particular, its effect comes from its tragicomic structure.

Commentators are agreed that O'Casey's own description of the play (in the subtitle) as a tragedy is misleading. Much of the play is broadly comic, even farcical, in style, though there are darker shades from the opening lines onwards. The undertones of violence and betrayal remain undertones, however, until the end of Act Two, and it is only in Act Three that catastrophe is on the agenda. And even there, even though financial failure, death, unwanted pregnancy and the break-up of the family all descend rapidly, the ending of the play returns to the comic mode. All of this volatility is somewhat puzzling, somewhat challenging. We should not take it for granted that the play is above criticism: on the contrary, we should note the defiance of conventional structure and genre and begin at that point to isolate O'Casey's originality and daring.

The London critic James Agate put his finger on an important clue to this contradiction in O'Casey's dramaturgy when, in reviewing the London production in 1925, he wrote: '*Juno and the Paycock* is as much a tragedy as *Macbeth*, but it is a tragedy taking place in the porter's family.' In other words, since Shakespeare's porter is a comic character, O'Casey structures his tragedy around comic individuals. It is the *juxtaposition* which ignites the explosion creating the devastating effect the play can have on readers and spectators alike. The most obvious and undoubtedly the most daring example occurs in Act Two, where the Boyle party goes on simultaneously with the Tancred funeral. The clash of moods here is devastating. Mrs Tancred's loss is as tragic for her as the murder of Duncan in *Macbeth* is for his sons; but in *Macbeth* we do not have the porter's family celebrating anything at just this time. O'Casey, by yoking comedy and tragedy together at this point, is insisting that 'in the midst of life we are in death, but in the midst of death we are in life also'. The mixture creates a scalding, tough-minded irony.

One might say the same thing about the ending of *Juno*: the entrance of Captain Boyle and Joxer Daly, blind-drunk, is bound to raise a laugh just after Juno's magnificent speech which raised the play to the heights of great tragedy. Some of the early reviewers thought this 'coda', this additional scene (as they saw it) of Boyle and Joxer ruined the tragic impact: O'Casey, they asserted, had made 'a painful mistake' (Lawrence, p. 88). It is a point worth arguing about, for O'Casey deliberately challenges us with the ending he chose. Gabriel Fallon, who played Charles Bentham in the first production of *Juno*, was emphatic that the drunken epilogue was a stroke of genius and told O'Casey so. It seems that because O'Casey had already been persuaded to cut a scene in which the death of Johnny was shown onstage, he was not entirely confident that the last scene was right either. Clearly, however, O'Casey *knew* it was right immediately he saw it work onstage.

Yet the ending remains a challenge, since its effect is to sweep away tragic feeling and bury it in laughter. Not only does life reassert itself through the comedy, but as a result of the *contrast* with Juno's expression of suffering and endurance the essential sterility of Boyle's fantasies is brought clearly into the light. It is a complex ending, then, which forces us to think and to judge as well as to laugh.

Action and Themes

Something has already been said about O'Casey's use of contrast. It is necessary now to comment on the three plots which comprise the action of *Juno* and to see how they fuse into a tragicomic design. There is Johnny's story (orginally intended to be the main one), Mary's story, and the story of the legacy. Johnny's story is backgrounded, Mary's foregrounded, and yet both are based on a similar theme: betrayal. Johnny is a traitor, if we insist on judging him morally, and his guilt makes him resemble Macbeth, at least in his dread of the supernatural and his inability to rest: 'I can rest nowhere, nowhere, nowhere.' (p. 103). Where Donal Davoren in *The Shadow of a Gunman* only wanted to be 'on the run' in order to gain himself more privacy, Johnny Boyle offers a portrait of a man genuinely on the run, terrorised, in flight from all the consequences of his actions: in flight from history itself.

Johnny is marginalised from the family, his crippled status more often driving him offstage to his bedroom and safety than allowing him to participate in the hustle and bustle of family life. His visible action is retreat; his secret action is to cause the death of Robbie Tancred and thus cause his own death by reprisal. Where Johnny is in retreat, Mary, resembling Minnie Powell in *The Shadow of a Gunman*, is proactive. In discarding Jerry Devine as suitor she chooses Bentham. She chooses an illusion, just as Johnny did. And equally she is a victim. Like Johnny, Mary declares she lives by 'principle', especially the principle of dedication to solidarity, to the welfare of comrades. But the play shows how useless 'principle' is in the face of chance, error, and what Juno calls 'the stupidity o' men' (p. 145).

These two plots, then, run into the sand. The motives of both Johnny and Mary are brushed aside callously by forces indifferent to their personal ambitions. In the opening stage-direction O'Casey makes clear how much environment has to do with this destruction. The environment creates a trap from which there is no escape for Johnny; only through Juno's heroic intervention is Mary liberated, at a cost to the family unit.

The third plot, the legacy, is the controlling one so far as the fortunes of the Boyle family are concerned. It is sometimes said that the legacy which falls through is nothing but a melodramatic device, a creaky plot-mechanism borrowed from popular theatre. But this time it is based on a true story which happened to one John Moore, a man in O'Casey's apartment block in 1921. A surviving letter reveals how O'Casey wrote to a solicitor to see if Moore could be helped towards the promised inheritance (*Letters*, vol. i, pp. 92–3). The will had been made out incorrectly, by a schoolmaster, as in the play. O'Casey often used incidents from real life in this way as the material of his plays, but it happens sometimes, as we know, that truth is stranger than fiction, and to some people the legacy story in *Juno* still remains unconvincing. If we see it as symbolic, however, its real impact may more easily be registered.

The sudden stroke of good luck which raises the hopes of the Boyle family, only for them to be cruelly dashed, is the sort of event which in tragedy would be called the work of fate. It is a universal occurrence symbolising the human need to dream, to hope for deliverance through some miraculous intervention. What else does the National Lotto promise? Why else did Macbeth suddenly respond to the witches' promise of fufilled ambition? But the Boyles are unlucky: they won and then they lost everything. It was a cruel blow, an accident, something unplanned by Bentham: the sort of thing which ought not to but can happen. The way it affects the Boyle family is what matters. It clearly interacts with Captain Boyle's characteristic weakness, his reliance on fantasy (to be discussed below), and seems to inflate Mary's expectations from Bentham.

Bentham's error in making out the will causes his flight, although Mary never sees it like that. The legacy, however, makes no difference at all to Johnny's situation. It may be that the celebratory party, recklessly held on the very day when Tancred's body is to be taken to church, sent the wrong signal to the IRA, who come at this point to summon Johnny to answer the charge of betraying Tancred. Certainly to an outsider the Boyles' insensitive partying must have appeared like dancing on Tancred's grave, and it may have activated Johnny's nemesis, but this point is not made in the text. O'Casey preferred to show Johnny's pursuit and eventual arrest by the IRA as the working out of the inevitable consequence of Johnny's own guilt. This would have happened regardless of the legacy – which is, then, mainly the outward sign of an inner tragic design in this family's affairs.

The loss of the legacy reinforces a major theme in the play, a theme picked up in the other two plots also: the conflict between dream and reality. The news brings the family down to earth with a sickening impact. At this point, in Act Three, reality asserts itself and in so doing ushers in what may be seen as another defining theme: chaos, or what Boyle repeatedly miscalls 'chassis'.

The disorder which overwhelms the action derives centrally from the civil war. What greater chaos can there be within society than civil war? In Book 4 of his autobiography, O'Casey has a chapter headed 'Into Civil War' which describes how the fight began in Dublin between the Free Staters and the Irregulars, or republicans, who rejected the Treaty approved by the people in 1921:

> Defeated in the Four Courts, the Republicans fortified themselves within a long portion of O'Connell Street [where Johnny Boyle had his arm blown off in the fighting]; and Business and Banking hurried everything valuable into their safes, before retiring to the country to wait till things settled down. Once more, machine-gun and rifle-fire, rising and falling and rising again, shivered the air into a sharp and bitter moaning, pierced now and then by the strident bark of a ten-pounder sending snarling protests into buildings housing the deadliest marksmen among the Republicans. Occasionally, the shrill squealing of the gun-fire was relieved by the gentle and more musical tinkle of falling glass, splitting away from trembling windows that now began to send out flickering tongues of flame growing swiftly into steady streams of burning destruction, till the smoky skyline was changed into a rosy and tumultuous lake of fire. (p. 93)

It is a magnificent description, very useful as background reading. The 'lake of fire' is a picture of hell. The details

of the murders and retaliations which tore Dublin apart
led O'Casey to conclude: 'the whole of Ireland's following
horses these days ... and Ireland herself's driving the
hearse' (p. 99). In a succeeding chapter, 'Comrades', he
tells of how a republican is brutally executed by a former
comrade, now in the Free State army: it is a carbon copy
of what happens to Johnny Boyle in *Juno*.

In *Juno*, O'Casey was thus writing from reality, which
itself was hellish. He was applying directly to Dublin that
expression of moral, civic and political breakdown which
Yeats had expressed in 'The Second Coming' (1921),
which was written following the Russian Revolution in
1917:

> Things falls apart; the centre cannot hold;
> Mere anarchy is loosed upon the world,
> The blood-dimmed tide is loosed, and everywhere
> The ceremony of innocence is drowned;

This sense of things falling apart is the 'chassis' of which
Captain Boyle so ludicrously complains.

The family tragedy, then, is set against the background
of a cruel, bloody and insidious civil war which registered
pure chaos. Yet the term 'background' is misleading.
What happens outside, in the streets of Dublin and in the
suburbs (the opening line of the play: 'On a little bye-
road, out beyant Finglas he [Tancred] was found'), soon
invades the very tenements of the poor. It is not background, then, but *mise-en-scène*, the very setting of the
action itelf. Juno tells us in Act Two that the whole
tenement in which the Boyles have two rooms has
suffered casualties: she lists four young men killed.
Johnny is soon to be the fifth and there is no end in
sight. The logic on which this relentless killing is based is

firmly supplied by the Young Man at the end of Act Two, come to order Johnny to appear at a meeting: 'Boyle, no man can do enough for Ireland!' (p. 121). The 'infernal machine' thus drives the action incessantly into chaos. Clearly, at last, that is why O'Casey insisted on subtitling the play 'a tragedy', in spite of the laughter that runs through it.

Characters

It is generally agreed that O'Casey's characterisation in *Juno* is what stamps the play with greatness. Lady Gregory had set him on the right path by insisting, 'Mr Casey, your gift is characterisation' rather than ideas (p. 75). She warned him off propaganda, towards which his earliest, rejected plays were inclined.

Captain Boyle and Joxer Daly go together like Laurel and Hardy: one is foil to the other in a continuing farce. It is proper to say 'farce' here in spite of the case just made for interpreting *Juno* as a dramatisation of chaos: in short, as tragedy. Boyle and Joxer refuse to recognise this tragedy, even though it is Boyle who constantly speaks of the whole world being in a state of 'chassis'. He has managed to insulate himself from this perception, if it *is* a perception and not just another piece of his humbug. For Boyle inhabits a fantasy world. Discontented with the identity conferred on him by birth and actual experience, he has constructed the persona of a sea-captain and dresses accordingly. He frequently uses nautical language; he plays his adopted role to the full. When the talk swings round to where the family might move to on the strength of the legacy, Boyle announces: 'I'm looking for a place near the sea; I'd like the place that you might say was me

cradle, to be me grave as well. The sea is always callin'
me' (p. 111). Yet we have Juno's word for it that Boyle
was only *once* at sea in his life, in an old coal ship from
Dublin to Liverpool! The rest is lies. We laugh at Boyle
for the liar and fantasist he is, because we recognise the
'paycock' in him, the type who, like Shakespeare's
Falstaff, can create fun and diversion just because of his
bare-faced lies. But Boyle is also irresponsible just as
Falstaff is irresponsible, and has finally to be rejected if
the serious business of living is to go forward.

Boyle's irresponsibility is seen in two major examples.
The first is when the party is in full swing in Act Two and
Juno suddenly remembers Mrs Tancred's grief. Boyle has
no regrets about this jollity in the circumstances: 'We've
nothin' to do with these things, one way or t'other. That's
the Government's business, an' let them do what we're
payin' them for doin'' (p. 116). The last part of this
sentence, born of Boyle's incorrigible pomposity, is bound
to raise one more laugh because Boyle more often *lives off*
government assistance than contributes any taxes. But the
laugh cannot abolish the callousness of the preceding
sentence. Boyle's indifference to the troubles around him
is entirely shocking. Even when Juno points out how close
these troubles are he hastens to dismiss them: 'that's
enough about them things; they don't affect us, an' we
needn't give a damn' (p. 117). He goes on to say that when
he was a sailor he was 'always resigned to meet with a
wathery grave', and by the same token those who insist on
fighting must be prepared to 'meet a soldier's fate'. This
rationalisation is nothing but escapism, for if we are to be
human, 'no man is an island,' and we must feel others'
loss and pain as if it were our own.

The other example is Boyle's reaction to the news of

Mary's pregnancy, which is to think of himself and not of Mary: 'Oh, isn't this a nice thing to come on top o' *me*, an' the state *I'm* in!' (p. 134, emphasis added). He is worried only about his own public image. So furious is he on this score that he blames Mary's disgrace on her reading: 'What did th' likes of her, born in a tenement house, want with readin'?' (p. 134). It is as if he believes ignorance is bliss. His attitude is narrow-minded and reactionary. This brutal side of him is a revelation to Juno and motivates her final decision to leave him and take Mary with her.

So, although we are amused by Boyle's vanity and '*self-honouring*' (p. 73) attitude all through the play, we must judge him harshly also or else we fail to register the play's deeper meaning. O'Casey himself described Boyle as 'an Irish Narcissus', self-absorbed and irresponsible, 'intent on his personal glory' (Rollins, p. 121). The ending, otherwise, will leave us untouched. For there we see the same old Boyle, drunken, steeped in a fantasy in which he plays a heroic role, while he is blissfully unaware of the tragedy all around him. It is funny when he says that the chairs will have to steady themselves (in the final scene), but we also recognise that here Boyle is projecting onto the furniture his own moral instability. In his final fantasy Boyle pretends he was out in Easter 1916 and came shoulder-to-shoulder with heroism. But his picture is entirely sentimental, the very opposite of the terror-stricken reality just then experienced by Johnny. The irony of this contrast throws Boyle's role-playing into a very sombre light.

Joxer Daly's role is as the Captain's parasite. Whether or not O'Casey was aware at this time – for he had already read widely – of the importance of the parasite figure in Roman comedy, he certainly managed to recycle the character for modern audiences. The parasite is essentially a clever flatterer. Exploiting the vanity and stupidity of his patron, whom he serves, he both makes a good living for himself and enjoys himself in the process. In English comedy the role tended to merge with the clown on the one hand and the medieval 'Vice' character (a two-faced trickster) on the other. Such characters were witty, subversive figures, mischief-makers who gave delight in proportion to their powers of survival.

O'Casey's Joxer is a variation of this stock type. That he has no position in Boyle's household is obvious: we are not talking now of a patron–servant relationship (as in Ben Jonson's *Volpone* (1606) for instance), for O'Casey's play is set among the lower classes. Outside the ambit of Boyle's need for an audience, Joxer has no role in society. Juno treats him as a scavenger and chases him at every opportunity; she fears his negative influence. The others simply ignore Joxer and he them. He exists as Boyle's shadow and no further; it is as if he were an extension of Boyle's personality, the projection of Boyle's need for an approving witness. Their relationship is symbiotic.

On his introduction Joxer is described as dried-up and prematurely aged, as if from a life-time of rat-like scavenging. His eyes have a *'cunning twinkle'* and his manner is *'ingratiating'*, eager to please; he is constantly smiling. He is quite clever, and often refers to books he has read. Yet at the party his cleverness is seen as quite superficial. Joxer is the Captain's sounding-board, forever echoing Boyle's self-pleasing sentiments. At times he has to back-track rapidly to accommodate Boyle's change of opinion, as over the role of the clergy in Irish history.

Having heard Boyle's anti-clericalism in Act One, Joxer is all set in Act Two to sing the same tune, only to discover that Boyle, now (as he thinks) elevated in class, no longer despises the clergy. At first wrong-footed, Joxer quickly recovers: 'You're takin' me up wrong, Captain,' and he begins to praise Father Farrell as 'a daarlin' man' (p. 100). This quick-wittedness is Joxer's strength. He knows that Boyle needs him as much as Joxer needs Boyle: all he has to do is bide his time, revise his story as he goes, and avail himself of whatever benefit Boyle scatters in his way as crumbs from the master's table.

There isn't much dignity in Joxer's position but he has the occasional satisfaction of revenge on his patroniser. Thus at the end of Act One, humiliated by Boyle's treatment, Joxer speaks his mind and exposes Boyle's hypocrisy: 'I have to laugh every time I look at the deep-sea sailor; an' a row on a river ud make him sea-sick!' (p. 96). He adds a further dig about Boyle's reluctance to work. These are truthful barbs, and Joxer's role is partly to show Boyle up as a sham, 'infernal rogue an' damned liar' (p. 132). But of course as parasite his main role is to flatter Boyle's vanity, and this he does constantly and amusingly, just as a 'feed' allows his comic counterpart onstage the opportunity to score against him.

In the end Joxer has to bear some responsibility for Boyle's refusal to face reality. He never once urges caution or advises the Captain positively: the very idea is ludicrous, for Joxer would not dare point this great man in the path of righteousness. As opportunist he is interested only in self-help. Joxer benefits from Boyle's foolish generosity when Boyle borrows money, and yet he shamelessly steals Boyle's last bottle of stout when the tide of fortune turns, blatantly lies through his teeth and accuses Nugent of the deed. His loyalty is comically limited to his own stomach. In the final scene we see that nothing has changed, that this 'butty' of Boyle's will remain a drinking companion and a parasite, just so long as Boyle's funds last. Since Boyle is already down to his last sixpence ('tanner') of borrowed money, the writing is ominously on the wall. The rat is about to leave the sinking ship.

Juno is clearly depicted as heroic in a world of anti-heroes and fools. She is the bread-winner, for not only is Boyle chronically unemployed and determined to remain so, but Johnny is unfit to work and Mary is on strike. Her attitude towards strikes and the bosses is surprisingly conservative: she is against the sympathetic strike. She cannot see why Mary should walk out in support of the likes of Jenny Claffey: 'up to this you never had a good word for her' (p. 70). The abstract notion of solidarity means nothing to Juno. Yet O'Casey, who as a Larkinite recognised the importance of the sympathetic strike if justice is to be achieved in worker–employer relations, in no way puts Juno down for her short-sighted view. It is the same when Johnny also starts to preach about the importance of 'principle' with regard to the fight for Irish freedom: 'Ah, you lost your best principle, me boy, when you lost your arm; them's the only sort o' principles that's any good to a workin' man' (p. 93). Conservative she may be, but Juno is a rock of common sense. She rejects all theory in favour of practicality.

Yet Juno is the one who *thinks* in the play; it is she rather than Boyle or Mary (who reads Ibsen) who repeatedly puzzles over the way politics or religion is developing: 'With all our churches an' religions, the worl's not a bit the better' (p. 104). Boyle refuses to debate the point and tries to return her to her traditional role of servant to the men ('Tay!'). She stands her ground, however, and insists on her point: that if people acted out their religious beliefs better, the world would improve. Again, when the subject of Irish politics and violence comes up she has an independent, humanistic view. She deplores the loss of young lives incurred by the civil war; hers is the only voice raised in condemnation of violence in the play.

On the other hand, there can be no doubt but that the representation of Juno is a gendered one. O'Casey's admiration for strong providing women, like his own mother, Susan, lends a certain amount of conventionality to his portraiture. Juno is the mother, the nurturer, the keeper of harmony in the home, the long-suffering wife, and so on. It would be interesting to look at her today from a feminist perspective: is she what might be called a 'door-mat'? She is first described as a woman bearing '*a look of listless monotony and harassed anxiety*' (p. 68) as a result of the endless economic struggle she endures, although it is added that she also exudes an air of '*mechanical resistance*'. O'Casey is trying to be truthful and at the same time to create a woman of spirit. Juno is the prisoner of an endemic situation, but at the same time she has developed ways of asserting herself by exposing Boyle's stratagems for maintaining the status quo. In particular, she ridicules the pains in his legs as an inadequate excuse for unemployment.

Juno stands up to Boyle so resolutely, indeed, that he insists, "Tisn't Juno should be her pet name at all, but Deirdre of the Sorras, for she's always grousin" (p. 73). In fact, the mythic Deirdre is named 'of the Sorrows' because of the misfortunes she has to *endure*, so Boyle's joke is more appropriate than he knows. If the major theme in the play is disorder, Juno sees her role as trying at all times to introduce and maintain order domestically. To do that she must oppose Boyle's laziness, Joxer's parasitism, Johnny's irritability and Mary's vanity. She is thus by no means a 'door-mat' but a strong, assertive woman.

Juno can be tender-hearted also, as in her concern for Johnny and his needs. She does not know what is at the root of his terror, but she does what she can to assuage it. For example, in Act Two we have this exchange:

MRS BOYLE: (*arranging table for tea*) You didn't look at our new gramophone, Johnny?

JOHNNY: 'Tisn't gramophones I'm thinking of.

MRS BOYLE: An' what is it you're thinkin' of, allanna? [my child]

JOHNNY: Nothin', nothin', nothin'.

MRS BOYLE: Sure, you must be thinkin' of somethin'; it's yourself that has yourself the way y'are; sleepin' wan night in me sisther's, an' the nex' in your father's brother's — you'll get no rest goin' on that way.

JOHNNY: I can rest nowhere, nowhere, nowhere.

MRS BOYLE: Sure, you're not thryin' to rest anywhere.

JOHNNY: Let me alone, let me alone, let me alone, for God's sake. (pp. 102–103).

Juno is made to appear nagging when she is really searching for ways to help. Her tenderness is apparent when she soothes him during the 'haunting' incident. Juno follows a firm line with Mary in Act One but, being fully mesmerised by Bentham, takes it for granted he will marry Mary. His upward mobility should be enough to carry Mary forward socially, so Juno rather fawns on him and struggles to impress him. When this turns out to be a mistake Juno, having taken medical action, now takes a different kind of action in confronting Boyle on Mary's behalf. Just before this occurs, however, we see Juno and Mary like sisters in Act Two, doing the duet 'Home to Our Mountains' (p. 112).

Juno's forgetting Mrs Tancred's grief is perhaps strange, but understandable, and as soon as she hears Mrs Tancred coming down the stairs she stops Boyle from using the gramophone and has the door opened to give light for the descent. Juno says later that perhaps she was not sufficiently sympathetic towards Mrs Tancred: why did she feel that pang? What more could she have done than offered a hot cup of tea? Perhaps she remembered the morbid interest they all showed in the spectacle of the funeral ('Here's the hearse, here's the hearse!' p. 120), and the run to the street to get a better view. Or perhaps it was the resumption of the party after Mrs Tancred's exit, necessitating Needle Nugent's reprimand about respect for the dead, leading in turn to Juno's sniffy response: 'Maybe, Needle Nugent, it's nearly time we had a little less respect for the dead, an' a little more regard for the livin' (p. 119). Maybe this is where she fails. Some critics fault Juno for her insensitivity here, as if, like Boyle, she showed indifference to Mrs Tancred's sufferings.

In any case, the real effect of Juno's sense of guilt in Act Three is that now, following her own son's murder, she can feel for all those who suffer and not just for any individual or for herself:

Maybe I didn't feel sorry enough for Mrs Tancred when her poor son was found as Johnny's been found now – because he was a Die-hard! Ah, why didn't I

remember that then he wasn't a Diehard or a Stater, but
only a poor dead son! (p. 146)

When she repeats Mrs Tancred's prayer here she alters it
from 'Mother o' God, have pity on the pair of us!' (Mrs
Tancred and neighbour Mrs Manning) to 'Mother o'
God, have pity *on us all*!' (p. 146, emphasis added).
Through the rest of this prayer, a repetition of Mrs
Tancred's words, Juno identifies with the other woman
and through her speaks for all – including the audience.

It follows that Juno is the main character in the play,
towering in significance and moral authority above any of
the men. Her final exit, we should be aware, is a defiant
gesture, for she turns her back on her marriage. Ibsen had
allowed Nora Helmer to do just this in *A Doll's House*
(1879), so the gesture was not entirely original, and yet in
the context of Irish drama set in the tenements O'Casey's
was a far greater challenge to conventional morality than
was Ibsen's. Juno's choice, her decision to leave Boyle to
stew in his own juice, has nothing romantic about it: she
does not leave to find herself or work things out for
herself intellectually but to look after Mary and the
expected baby in a practical way. Her decision is thus
entirely humanistic and in line with the great love she has
shown all through the play for those around her. When
she says, to counter Mary's despair that the baby will
have no father, 'It'll have what's far betther – it'll have
two mothers' (p. 146), Juno sweeps aside the popular
prejudice (to borrow Lady Bracknell's phrase) in favour
of two parents.

The conservative Juno is thus subversive in her own
determined way. And to the last she maintains her
woman's independent voice: 'Ah, what can God do agen

[against] the stupidity o' *men*! (p. 145, emphasis added). It is men rather than women who have caused the trouble in and around the Boyle household. Juno is feminist enough to see this, to use it as analysis of her situation, and to rebuild her life accordingly.

The other characters in the play – Mary, Johnny, Jerry Devine, Charles Bentham, Mrs Madigan and Needle Nugent – are all well-drawn but minor figures. It is possible to see Mary and Mrs Madigan as extending O'Casey's representation of women as tougher and more resilient than men. Mrs Madigan, while a gem of a role for an actress, is hardly more than a caricature of a gossipy neighbour. And yet the point is made that she is also a tough, sharp-witted and resourceful woman well able to survive in a man's world (as it was in the 1920s). On the other hand, Mary is doomed to fall.

Like Minnie Powell in *The Shadow of a Gunman*, Mary is ambitious but held back by her environment, as the opening stage-direction makes clear: '*Two forces are working in her mind – one, through the circumstances of her life, pulling her back; the other, through the influence of books she has read, pushing her forward*' (p. 67). Mary is the victim of both of these forces. The dynamic which leads her to dress well and to take an interest in books also drives her to drop Jerry Devine and take up with Charles Bentham, in whom she is much deceived. In all of these choices Mary thinks she is bettering herself, but there is a recklessness in her character also which makes her burn her bridges too soon. Perhaps her brother is being cynical when he tells her in Act Three that she should have kept her pregnancy secret from Jerry Devine and so make the best of a new situation, but Mary is too straight, too honest, so she hides nothing and Jerry comes off second-best through his patronising response to her halting confession. She will not lie to better herself.

And so Mary wins our respect, while Jerry is seen as a conventional and priggish, upwardly mobile sentimental-ist, unworthy to polish Mary's boots. He dares to ask her, 'My God, Mary, have you fallen as low as that?' (p. 140). In one sentence the narrowness of his moral view is exposed, and her superiority is established. On the other hand, the element of self-improvement in Mary blinds her to Bentham's worthlessness, for if he is cultured he is also weak. He proves this by running from his responsibilities, and yet when, at the start of Act Three, Juno forces Mary to say why Bentham has left her, she can only stammer, 'I don't know ... I don't know, mother ... only I think ... I imagine ... he thought ... we weren't ... good enough for him' (p. 123). This infuriates Juno, of course, who has none of Mary's shame of her origins. But Mary's ambition is tainted with snobbery and thus she is vulnerable to Bentham's qualifications. She loved him, however, and that, in a way, is her tragedy. O'Casey here presents a common occurrence and yet one that seems inevitable, given the two forces to which Mary falls victim.

Language

'In *Juno*', the critic Raymond Williams has remarked, 'the dominant action is the talk of Boyle and Joxer: idle talk, with a continual play at importance.' As an O'Casey character might have said, 'Them words are true, Mr Williams, and in another way they're not true.' On the one hand, there is a lot more action in *Juno* than the gab of Boyle and Joxer amounts to: as we have seen above, this is one of O'Casey's best-constructed plays, built along the lines of the well-made play in three acts and climaxing with the removal of Johnny Boyle for execution just at the time when the Two Furniture-removal Men are stripping the house bare and leaving the empty space as image of the desolation visited upon the Boyle family. So, it would not be accurate to suggest that *Juno* is a play like one of Chekhov's, all talk and little action. The underlying threat is present at all times, ticking like a time-bomb which goes off as planned in Act Three.

On the other hand, there is no question but that much of the interest in the play focuses on the entertaining exchange between those two old codgers, Captain Boyle and Joxer Daly. What they indulge in *is*, quite often, 'idle talk' with a pseudo-weightiness which is a form of 'play'. A prime example is the passage in Act One where Joxer reminds Boyle of the 'young days' (p. 88), when Boyle was supposedly a sailor enduring hurricanes at sea. The speech is prompted by the offstage call of the Coal Vendor (who eventually enters), because by association of ideas Joxer remembers that Boyle was once on a coal ship between Dublin and Liverpool, though he takes care to avoid mentioning this. In other words, the stage is set for Boyle's ensuing fantasy about what it was like on board ship, sailing from the Gulf of Mexico to the Antarctic. In describing the winds and the waves, he borrows un-ashamedly from Charles Dickens's *Dombey and Son*, where (in Chapter 49) Captain Cuttle reminisces in similar vein: 'Them's the times, my beauty, when a man may say to his messmate (previously a overhauling of the wollume), "a stiff-nor'-wester's blowing, Bill; hark, don't you hear it roar now!"', and describes a ship 'left to the mercy of the storm as had no mercy but *blowed* harder and harder yet, while the waves dashed over her, and beat her in' (p. 691, emphasis added). Dickens's Captain Cuttle provides O'Casey's Captain Boyle with a model, a prototype. But because Captain Cuttle himself is an eccentric, a lovable caricature of the British nineteenth-century sailor, O'Casey's, or rather Boyle's, imitation is decidedly theatrical, fashioned not from life but from literature. The language Boyle uses when he gets into full flight, then, is a long way from the language of daily life. It is the invention of a man who is an escapist. The philosophical questions, 'what is the stars?' and 'what is the moon?' (pp. 88–9) are sheer nonsense, but glorious nonsense. Joxer chimes in on cue, sustaining the illusion that the pair of them are immersed in weighty considerations. The arrival of the Coal Vendor, interrupting their fine thoughts, brings them down to earth with a bang and reminds us how fanciful the whole exchange is.

It may seem laborious to explore this passage in such detail, when it is plainly fanciful, but we have here a key to an important aspect of the language in *Juno*. It is theatricalised, in the sense that both Boyle and Joxer repeatedly invent a style of speech borrowed from books or plays or songs, and invent other voices as a form of inner dialogue. Their whole speech-pattern is thus a form of secondary playmaking. Another brief example is when Boyle hints to Joxer that the foreman of a job in Killester has invited them down, Joxer quickly catches the prompt and invents dialogue: 'Yis. "Come down on the blow o' dinner", says he, "an' I'll start you, an' any friend you like to brin' with you"' (p. 75). The Russian critic Mikhail Bahktin would call this technique the use of 'dialogic imagination'. It is a comic means of including a range of voices within a single speech. It is, as Raymond Williams says, a form of 'play', of improvisation in particular, but it is play as a means of subverting purposeful statement.

Another way of making the same point is to describe O'Casey's language as 'poetic' or 'neo-Elizabethan', a fairly common description by early commentators. The American critic John Gassner referred to O'Casey's reckless generosity with language, his 'prodigality', in contrast to the bare realism adopted by so many modern playwrights. As has already been emphasised in the commentary on *The Shadow of a Gunman*, O'Casey was never entirely committed to realism. He wanted truth onstage, certainly; he wanted the speech of the people and not some pseudo-literary discourse. And so he took the Dublin dialect and – just as Synge did with rural Irish speech-patterns – elaborated and exaggerated its basic mannerisms. Gassner argues that O'Casey's language is like the Elizabethans' (even though it is in prose) because of the love of rhetoric all characters display. 'It subsists on excess' (Gassner, p. 117). It is a kind of music, with a special rhythm discoverable only when the language is spoken aloud.

An example would be Boyle's habit of using a succession of rhetorical questions. One question might do so far as the *meaning* is concerned, but Boyle is more interested in the *effect*. He expands the sentences so that the phrasing builds up to an impressive climax usually containing a vivid image. Thus when he turns on Jerry Devine for betraying to Juno that he was in a pub, though he swore the contrary, Boyle demands: 'What business is it o' yours whether I was in a snug or no? What do you want to be gallopin' about afther me for? Is a man not to be allowed to leave his house for a minute without havin' a pack o' spies, pimps an' informers cantherin' at his heels?' (p. 79). In Irish political discourse, no term is more abusive than 'informer', with its roots in Irish history and the despised practice of selling secrets to the British forces of occupation. Boyle exaggerates his complaint until he presents himself as pursued by a whole *pack* of 'spies, pimps an' informers' snapping at his 'heels': the image of predatory animals is graphic, and, of course, insulting. All through the play Boyle uses these techniques – rhetorical questions, repetition, alliteration and hyperbole. His language is figurative and vivid.

Boyle is not alone, of course, in using a poetic style. It is within the range of all the characters – even of minor figures such as Mrs Madigan and Needle Nugent. They are all in love with words and can elaborate them to devastating effect. The conclusion is that these characters invest all their energy into words rather than deeds. If this is what Raymond Williams means (see above) then he is right: action is not available to the working class, especially while a dangerous civil war is raging in the streets, and so they take refuge in language. Or they use it as 'a kind of rebellion', to quote Jack Mitchell's phrase – a rebellion, that is, against the accountability and responsibility a disordered society imposes. It is a language of 'poetry in revolt' (Ellis-Fermor).

It has already been explained, in the section on the language of *The Shadow of a Gunman*, that O'Casey's language is Hiberno-English; it assimilates Gaelic words, Gaelic syntax and the forms of English used in Ireland since the seventeenth century. For that reason O'Casey's English is bound to appear exotic when measured by the norms of standard English. For example, he uses 'a gradle' (a great deal), 'ower that' (out of that), 'collogin' (conspiracy), 'allanna' (baby), 'bellows'd' (broadcast), and so on. Phrases denoting the perfect tense commonly follow the Hiberno-English form, influenced by Gaelic grammar, e.g., Boyle's 'he must have afther lifted' (Nugent 'must have taken'), or Joxer's reply, 'Ah no, ah no; he wouldn't be afther doin' that now' ('he wouldn't have done'). Malapropisms are used to good effect: not only Boyle's 'chassis' (chaos), but 'pereeogative' (prerogative), 'suspicious' (auspicious), 'to commensurate' (to mensurate or measure) and 'formularies' (formalities).

An additional factor is accent or pronunciation, sometimes rendered by phonetic spelling, which gives the flavour of Dublin speech and speech rhythms. Here O'Casey may have been indebted to Shaw, who in *Major Barbara* (1906) and *Pygmalion* (1913) reproduced cockney speech for comic effect.

Performance

Juno and the Paycock has, since its première on 3 March 1924, been consistently popular on stage. 'Scarcely a year goes by without a production of it somewhere' (Schrank, p. 40), and indeed in the year of its seventy-fifth anniversary in 1999 there were *two* major productions, in Dublin (Gaiety) and London (Donmar). The first London production was in November 1925 and the New York première in March 1926. The success of the play internationally has had a great deal to do with the Abbey style of playing. Indeed, when Laurence Olivier revived the play in April 1966 (National Theatre) he wrote in a programme note that he saw the first London production when he was about eighteen and never forgot its impact. The players he saw then became his 'worshipped heroes' (p. 90). One of those players, Harry Hutchinson, who played Johnny Boyle, was assistant director to Olivier in the 1966 production and thus ensured the transmission of authentic stage-business. Olivier's production was outstanding. It probably re-established *Juno* as a classic play of the twentieth century.

As with *The Shadow of a Gunman*, it is necessary to understand how theatrical *Juno and the Paycock* is. 'Dramatic' is one thing – we can easily see how the opening of *Juno* is dramatic in the sense that it sets up a situation whereby a man has been brutally murdered and Johnny Boyle seems very upset at the news – but 'theatrical' is another matter. We are here concerned with details of performance, and Mary reading aloud from the newspaper before Juno enters focuses our attention on the vital detail of the murder before we get swept into more immediate details of family life.

Just twelve lines after Juno enters, Johnny exits to his room. Entrances and exits, when and how they take place, are also vital in performances. Juno enters from shopping; the image of provider is thus immediately given. Had the play opened with Juno in her apron at the kitchen table that particular image would be less vivid. Johnny's rapid exit in reaction to Mary's reading aloud from the news-paper creates curiosity – onstage, action always speaks louder than words and Johnny's outburst means less than his flight to the refuge of his room: we see that he is scared. He will enter and exit again a page and a half later. His call offstage for a drink of water leads to Juno's exit and re-entry. A lot of activity takes place within a few lines, establishing the dependency of these grown-up 'children' and this earth-mother figure. (The details of Johnny's injuries also make more impact when we see and hear how nervous he is.)

Other details from the opening scenes also indicate that

in reading this play we must not only absorb the stage-directions but imagine what they signify visually and in action (the proper theatrical term is 'semiotically'). Thus when Jerry Devine comes running in looking for 'the Captain', we are told that Mary Boyle *'seizes her jumper and runs hastily into the room left'* (p. 72). Now they were lovers up until recently, as emerges a little later, and yet Mary runs off as soon as Jerry enters. She *'seizes her jumper'* because she is partly embarrassed and, presumably, does not want to be seen in her underwear. But is it not significant that she does this? Is it not some kind of statement to Jerry? If she cared for him would she not have found a way of lingering to speak to him and still manage to cover herself up (or not, as she might decide)? She *'runs hastily'*, however, without saying a word. It is only later that we find out what lies behind her indifference, but what we, as readers, have to register here is the negative feelings Mary has for Jerry. This is how performance details can enrich our reading of the text.

In the famous reunion between O'Casey and Barry Fitzgerald in 1959 (recorded in the short film *Cradle of Genius*) O'Casey recalled Fitzgerald's first entry as Captain Boyle. What he remembered was the song. This is something we might not immediately register in the reading, but it shows again how important O'Casey's stage-directions are. Boyle and Joxer are still offstage when their footsteps are heard on the stairs and Boyle's voice is heard singing from a popular Irish opera the aria 'Sweet Spirit, hear my prayer' (p. 73). The song prepares us for his grand entrance, but we have to imagine how it would sound. It sets up an image of a cultured, music-loving figure. The second voice, Joxer's, praises the song but Juno, onstage, undercuts it *'viciously'* by mocking the sentiments: 'Sweet spirit hear his prayer!' Juno feels certain Boyle is not praying for a job in any event. The contrast between song and reception is comic and renders Boyle's entrance (while Juno hides) extremely dramatic. Of course, ever after in the play the Captain is liable to burst into song, and it is he who is master of ceremonies at the party in Act Two, so his singing is part of his character, at once carefree and ludicrous.

Enough has been said in the section above on characters to emphasise the point that Captain Boyle is always performing. He and Joxer do a constant double-act. They are masked against the world, like an odd couple or like the two tramps in Beckett's *Waiting for Godot* (1953). In this way they insulate themselves against the demands of domestic responsibility. Such evasion is comic, and in order to remain comic the 'performance' has to be maintained. Boyle's mask of the upstanding, knowledgeable, much-travelled man remains funny because when it slips we see the lazy, drink-loving, irresponsible head of the household. The contrast is laughable, but Boyle himself never acknowledges this. The actor playing the role has to play a man playing a double role without once conceding the point. This outrageous two-facedness is what sustains the comedy.

But as with *The Shadow of a Gunman* this play is a tragicomedy. O'Casey even went so far as to subtitle it 'a tragedy'. Therefore, in performance there must be a balance between the comic and the tragic elements. Often, this is a matter of casting. A very good, i.e. comic, Captain Boyle playing against as lively a soul mate as Joxer will overwhelm the play if the actress playing Juno is not sufficiently strong in the role. Mrs Madigan is a factor in this equation also because, though a minor part, hers is a very funny one for most of the play but then must switch to find deeper, tragic notes when she comes to tell Juno of Johnny's death. Mrs Madigan shows she has more to her than music-hall 'turns' when she voluntarily goes for a shawl for Mrs Tancred in Act Two, *'returns, and wraps a shawl around her'* (p. 115). It is in the action of wrapping the shawl around Mrs Tancred that Mrs Madigan's true humanity emerges. This gesture makes her believable in Act Three as sympathiser with Juno and a strong voice in getting the police to be more considerate.

Needless to say, the major scene where performance as such is transparently called for is the party scene in Act Two. Here, however, the shadow of Tancred's funeral falls heavily across the proceedings, and we must read the scene as compounded of an ironic blend of comedy and tragedy. The play calls for their juxtaposition at this point, after which the tragic note is increasingly dominant only to be ironically challenged by the final scene. The control of mood by director and performers is essential through all the scenes, but particularly from the party scene to the (literally) bitter end. As we read these scenes we should try to picture them in performance, letting O'Casey's stage-directions help us as much as possible.

In a revival of *Juno and the Paycock* at the Abbey in 1997–8, directed by Ben Barnes, the ending was reinterpreted in ways that show on the one hand the robustness of the play, its capacity to respond to new ways of looking at it, and on the other hand the effect of introducing changes onstage. In this production Juno was played by a youngish (not yet forty) actress, slim and good-looking, in defiance of the tradition that has Juno a middle-aged, careworn woman with no obvious sexual attractiveness. (The text says Juno is forty-five and was once *'a pretty woman*' (p. 68). In this strongly feminist production, Juno (Ger Ryan) was no 'shawlie', or traditional Irish washer-woman. With her hair piled on top of her head and her natural elegance she could be seen as Mary's mother, not vain but yet careful enough of her appearance. This was a Juno who refused to give in to the onslaughts of poverty. She was a great deal stronger and brighter than Captain Boyle (Vincent McCabe), and the balance of the play was decidedly in her favour.

At the end of what in the text is her last scene, Juno here stayed onstage, which was almost entirely bare, gathering up various bits and pieces after Mary had exited with Mrs Madigan. The actress came across the curtain which had screened Johnny's bed and in folding it was overcome with grief, while the folded curtain became a baby which she rocked in her arms. Meanwhile, Joxer and the Captain arrived on the stairs visible outside the room and, seeing Juno, remained on the stairs. Juno stayed stage-centre while the duo went through their drunken scene, and the spotlight stayed on her silent figure as the lights went down. Whereas this change went against the text, it was an effective way of carrying through the feminist reading of the play which margin-alised the men and kept Juno centre-stage. Thus the production challenged its audiences, and reception once again became a vital part of the play's energy.

Textual Notes

68 environment – social surroundings. The term was part of the vocabulary of naturalism, as it derived from the determinism of Charles Darwin. Compare 'circumstances' in the description of Juno.

- beyant – beyond.
- Finglas – suburb on Dublin's northside.
- paycock – peacock, proverbially proud. In Dublin pronunciation, the vowel-sound 'ea' becomes 'a'. Compare 'tay' below (tea).
- Diehard – name given to the members of the IRA who refused to accept the Treaty creating the Irish Free State in 1922.
69 good Samaritan – in the Bible, the stranger who gives charity to the man injured by robbers and left for dead (Luke 10: 30–36). The Good Samaritan is Christ's example of the good neighbour.
- Novena – in the Roman Catholic liturgy, nine days of special prayers for personal intentions.
71 Easter Week – reference to the 1916 Rising led by Pádraic Pearse and James Connolly.
- Fight in O'Connell Street – in 1920, during the Irish war of independence.
- Free State – established in 1922 after the Treaty signed between Ireland and Great Britain. Ireland became a republic in 1949.
72 snug – alcove or little room in a public house.
- give him a start – the phrase used in the building trade for 'give him a job'.
73 affeydavey – phonetic spelling of 'affidavit', a written statement confirmed by oath.
- furrage – forage, hunt out.
- Deirdre of the Sorras – 'Sorrows', the usual description of the mythical beautiful woman who deserted King Conchubar to run off, as prophesied, with Naisi, this bringing ruin and destruction on Ulster. AE, Yeats and Synge all wrote plays on Deirdre.

83

74 the cup that cheers – a quotation from the eighteenth-century poet William Cowper (1731–1800), which ends 'but not inebriate'. Joxer has a fund of such familiar quotations.

75 butty – friend (compare American 'buddy').

79 pereeogative – malapropism for 'prerogative', special right.

80 at wanst – at once.

82 hillabaloo – hullabaloo, loud noise.

83 Chiselurs – children (Dublin dialect).
 – chassis – chaos.
 – sassige – sausage.

84 e'er a – any.
 – thrench coat – a trench coat (gaberdine) was commonly worn by members of the IRA.

85 the bend – signal.
 – *The Doll's House, Ghosts*, an' *The Wild Duck* – Boyle mistakes Henrik Ibsen's tragic plays for children's books.
 – *Elizabeth, or Th' Exile o' Sibayria* – (i.e., of Siberia) a popular tale by Madame Sophil Cottin (1770–1807).

86 argufy – argue.
 – aself – itself, Hiberno-English, for emphasis (even).
 – brought up on Virol – i.e., not a child. The reference is to an advertisement for baby food.

87 oul' fella – father.
 – '47 – in 1847 the Great Famine was at its height.
 – Parnell – Charles Stewart Parnell (1846–91), known as 'the uncrowned king of Ireland', who fell from political favour when his affair with Katherine O'Shea was exposed.
 – Fenians – the Irish Republican Brotherhood,

founded in 1858 as a radical, militarist form of nationalism.

88 an' the wins blowin' fierce ... blowed – this passage seems indebted to Captain Cuttle's description of storms at sea in Charles Dickens's *Dombey and Son* (1848).

89 How can a man die ... gods? – lines from Thomas Macaulay's *Lays of Ancient Rome* (1842).

90 collogin' – conspiring (Hiberno-English).

93 Ireland only half free – a reference to the partition of Ireland introduced by the Treaty of 1921. It is clearly a slogan based on Pádraic Pearse's line, 'Ireland, unfree, shall never be at peace!' (oration over the grave of O'Donovan Rossa, 1915). Compare *The Plough and the Stars*, Act Two (p. 201).

94 Sorra many'll – not many, nobody (dialect, usage for emphatic negative).

95 N.T. – National Teacher.

– A wet – a drink (slang).

96 Requiescat in pace – may he rest in peace (Latin).

– Guh sayeree jeea ayera! – phonetic spelling for the prayer 'Go saoraigh Dia Eire!' (God save Ireland!)

98 attackey case – attaché case, meant to impress Joxer (though in production it may betray the clink of bottles!)

99 five bob – five shillings (old money), 25p, perhaps worth £20 today.

– I met with Napper Tandy – line from a ballad, 'The Wearing of the Green'. James Napper Tandy (1740–1803) was an Irish patriot.

100 the heart o' the rowl – O'Casey himself explained this Dublin expression as 'a jolly good fellow ... usually in drinking circles' (*Letters*, vol. iv, p. 168).

- Saggart Aroon – dear priest (Gaelic). In 1798, in particular, several priests were involved in the fight for freedom and songs were written about them.
- J. L. Sullivan – Boyle confuses the Irish-American prize-fighter with the Irish historian A. M. Sullivan, whose *Story of Ireland* (1870) went through many editions.

101 Boney's Oraculum – O'Casey's own explanation reads: 'a pamphlet sold [at] that time for a penny, containing interpretations of dreams; explanations of meaning of cards turned up when a fortune is being told, a book of signs & wonders, popular with the ignorant or superstitious: Book of Oracles' (*Letters*, vol. iv, p. 168).

102 allanna – my baby (Gaelic).

103 Consols – Government Securities (stocks).

109 no names, no pack dhrill – army phrase for 'keep silent'. O'Casey's own explanation: 'Pack drill was a military punishment in Victorian days ... phrase meant as an indication of caution about revealing something' (*Letters*, vol. iv, p. 168).

- puff – life (slang).

110 signs on it – the proof is clear (Hiberno-English).
Nil desperandum – never despair (Latin).

111 ball o' malt – glass of whiskey (Dublin slang).

- suspicious – malapropism for 'auspicious', i.e. of good omen, favourable.

112 '*Home to Our Mountains*' – aria from Verdi's *Il Trovatore* (1853).

113 shut-eyed wans – presumably, traditional songs ('ones').

- She is far from the lan' – one of the melodies of the

Irish poet and songwriter Thomas Moore (1779–1852).

114 mavis – thrush.

Whisht – be quiet! (Hiberno-English, possibly from the Gaelic *bí id'thost*).

116 hearts o' stone ... hearts o' flesh – based on a passage from the Bible, Ezekiel 11: 19 (Ayling, *Seven Plays*, glossary).

117 collandher – colander; a strainer in cookery.

118 copper – penny.

119 Civic Guards – Gardaí Síochána, the Irish police force.

124 Sorra mend you! – good enough for you!

125 *Messenger* – a pious Roman Catholic magazine.

126 get a dhrop – a setback, a disappointment.

– a red rex – a copper, a penny.

– a make – a halfpenny.

127 juice – twopence (Ayling, *Seven Plays*, glossary).

128 like a redshank – in a flash. O'Casey's own explanation was: 'a seagull with red legs, rarer than those with yellow ones ... staying anywhere only for a short time' (*Letters*, vol. iv, p. 168).

129 man's inhumanity ... mourn – a quotation from Robert Burns (1759–96).

130 formularies – malapropism for 'formalities'.

133 a gradle – a great deal.

– Child o' Mary – member of a Roman Catholic confraternity devoted to the Virgin Mary.

– bellows'd – broadcast, blown about.

136 a banjax – a mess. This slang word is usually a verb in the past participle, banjaxed (destroyed).

141 An' we felt the power ... out of tune – these lines were by O'Casey himself and, under the title 'A

Walk with Eros', were published with some
alterations in his *Windfalls* (1934).

143 Sean Boyle – the use of the Gaelic form of Johnny's
name is ominous.

– beads – rosary beads, which to a Roman Catholic
in Johnny's circumstances suggest he is about to
die.

144 mothor – motor car.

146 Take your hour – take your time (Dublin slang,
often 'hold your hour').

147 The last o' the Mohicans – his last (bit of money),
'the last one'; the expression derives from *The Last
of the Mohicans* (1826) by American novelist James
Fenimore Cooper (1789–1851).

– the blinds is down – O'Casey's own explanation:
'the end of things, the utter end; from the custom, I
imagine, of pulling down the blinds to darken a
house in which death has struck down a member of
the family living in it' (*Letters*, vol. iv, p. 168).

– Put all ... your throubles – 'Pack Up All Your
Troubles (in Your Old Kit-Bag)' was a popular song
from World War I.

– Irelan' sober is Irelan' free – the slogan of an Irish
temperance movement, here used ironically.

– a flyin' column – a guerilla or commando unit.

– Breathes there a man – from Walter Scott's poem
The Lay of the Last Minstrel (1805)

– Willie ... Reilly – a reference to William Carleton's
novel, *Willy Reilly and His Dear Colleen Bawn*
(1855). It has no apparent relevance.

References

Agate, James, 'Juno and the Paycock (1925)', in Sean O'Casey: Modern Judgements, ed. Ronald Ayling, London: Macmillan, 1969, pp. 76–8.

Ellis-Fermor, Una, The Irish Dramatic Movement, London: Methuen, 1954, p. 199.

Gassner, John, 'The Prodigality of Sean O'Casey (1951)', Sean O'Casey: Modern Judgements, ed. Ronald Ayling, London: Macmillan, 1969, pp. 110–19.

Gregory, Lady Augusta, Journals, ed. Lennox Robinson, London: Putnam, 1946, p. 75.

Lawrence, W. J., review of Juno and the Paycock (1924), in O'Casey: The Dublin Trilogy. A Casebook, ed. Ronald Ayling, London: Macmillan, 1985, pp. 87–9.

Malone, A. E., 'O'Casey's Photographic Realism (1929)', in Sean O'Casey: Modern Judgements, ed. Ronald Ayling, London: Macmillan, 1969, pp. 68–75.

Mitchell, Jack, 'Inner Structure and Artistic Unity (1980)', in O'Casey: The Dublin Trilogy. A Casebook, ed. Ronald Ayling, London: Macmillan, 1985, pp. 99–111.

O'Casey, Sean, Autobiography, Book 4: Inishfallen, Fare Thee Well, London, Pan, 1972.

– Letters, Volume I, 1910–41, ed. David Krause, London: Cassell, 1975.

– Letters, Volume IV, 1959–64, ed. David Krause, Washington DC: Catholic University of America Press, 1992.

Olivier, Laurence, 'Meditations on Juno and the Paycock', in O'Casey: The Dublin Trilogy. A Casebook, ed. Ronald Ayling, London: Macmillan, 1985, pp. 90–2.

Rollins, Ronald G., Sean O'Casey's Drama: Verisimilitude

and Vision, Alabama: University of Alabama Press, 1979, p. 121.

Schrank, Bernice, *Sean O'Casey: A Research and Production Sourcebook*, Westport, CT: Greenwood Press, 1996, p. 40.

Williams, Raymond, *Drama from Ibsen to Brecht*, Harmondsworth: Penguin, 1976, pp. 163–4.

Yeats, W. B., 'The Second Coming', in *Collected Poems of W. B. Yeats*, London: Macmillan, 1950, p. 211.

The Plough and the Stars

Introduction

Without a doubt, *The Plough and the Stars* is O'Casey's greatest play. It is the one with the greatest intensity, the one which most ambitiously addresses the human comedy at the point where violent public events suddenly transform it into tragedy. It is the O'Casey play which tackles the greatest Irish theme, the fight for freedom, and humanises it with searing irony to equal the greatest critiques of war and peace to be found in literature, from Shakespeare's *Henry IV* to Bertolt Brecht's *Mother Courage and Her Children*.

The Plough and the Stars was intended as a critique of the 1916 Rising, ten years on. By this time, the new Free State had got under way but in various elections the cause of Labour fell more and more behind. To one of O'Casey's socialist persuasion this signalled a betrayal of the workers' cause which he and Jim Larkin had striven to protect from 1913. When Jim Larkin returned from prison in the United States (where he had been sentenced as an 'anarchist' for preaching socialism) in 1923 he tried to regain control over the Irish trade-union movement and instead felt the full resistance of the new men, comfortable in their secure, non-militant organisation. Larkin was made to feel a total outsider, was charged with embezzling union funds years earlier, and had to create for himself a rival trade-union organisation in the late 1920s. All of this confirmed for the embittered O'Casey that the new state was founded on bourgeois and not Labour principles. Looking back, he saw that the 1916 Rising was the clue to the problem.

This rebellion, undertaken through an alliance between James Connolly (who replaced Larkin as leader of the trade-union movement and chief of the Irish Citizen Army when Larkin went to America in 1914) and Pádraic Pearse, a teacher, a poet, a devotee of the Irish language and a prominent officer in the Irish Volunteers, was a total disaster. It took place in confusion, since Pearse and his supporters acted in defiance of higher orders to cancel the rebellion, orders that were in all the Sunday newspapers the day before the planned action, Easter Monday 1916. The Rising was thus a minor affair, confined to Dublin, and involved some 1,600 Volunteers and 300 members of the Irish Citizen Army. Pearse was the commander-in-chief, and he it was who read the proclamation of the Irish republic outside the General Post Office. By Saturday of Easter week all was over and Pearse surrendered. He and fourteen other leaders (including Connolly) were put on trial for treason and executed in Kilmainham Jail in Dublin. They were quickly turned into martyrs by a population which had at first ridiculed the insurgents (the looting of shops in O'Connell Street which O'Casey depicts in *The Plough and the Stars* actually occurred, signifying the indifference of the poor people of Dublin to the lofty ideals proclaimed by Pearse across the street in the General Post Office). As the poet Yeats discerned (in 'Easter 1916'), all was changed, changed utterly by the executions and 'a terrible beauty was born'. As O'Casey read the situation, however, the 1916 Rising was the root of a succession of wars and acts of terror succeeded by the civil war of 1922–3, when those who had accepted the Treaty were opposed by those who saw it as a betrayal of 1916.

In O'Casey's analysis, the nationalist ideal was both romantic and dangerous. Labour's alliance with nationalism was, in his view, a tragic mistake which abandoned the cause of the poor and the unemployed. He was thus prepared to pour scorn on the whole 1916 endeavour as fatally misguided. Its representation onstage was to shock audiences ill-prepared for this kind of satire.

On the fourth night of its first production at the Abbey Theatre, in February 1926, *The Plough* was greeted by riots of a similar kind to those which greeted Synge's masterpiece *The Playboy of the Western World* in January 1907. The reception of O'Casey's masterpiece, accordingly, marked a crisis in the modern Irish theatre. Violent opposition to a playwright's vision threatens the very foundation on which art makes its stand, namely the free expression of individual feeling. O'Casey's vision resembled Synge's in this: both were satirists of pretence and hypocrisy. But O'Casey's point of view was far more political than Synge's and so the offence he caused to a section of the audience arose from his deliberate repudiation of nationalism whereas Synge, as W. B. Yeats memorably recorded, 'was unfitted to think a political thought'.

Since the circumstances of the opposition at the Abbey Theatre throw some light on the play itself it may be worthwhile to provide a few details here. The problem began with the second act, where the prostitute Rosie Redmond sets the scene in the public house. This was a shocking innovation in itself, and clearly O'Casey intended to bring together in a spirit of mockery patriotism (outside the public house) and prostitution (within). When a member of the Abbey Board had objected to the character of Rosie some months before the production, Yeats himself was firm in her defence: 'She is certainly as necessary to the general action and idea as are the drunkards and wastrels. O'Casey is contrasting the ideal dream [that is, the patriotic dream expressed by the Figure in the Window] with the normal grossness of life, and of that she [Rosie] is an essential part' (Lady Gregory, *Journals*). To his credit, Yeats insisted on Rosie's being left in the script. O'Casey's satire made itself felt on the audience as Act Two progressed: the words of Pádraic Pearse used by the Figure in the Window were recognised, and the contrast between their high-mindedness and the low life and vulgarity of the working-class characters in the pub became increasingly obvious. The climax came when the three men in uniform, Clitheroe, Langan and Brennan, entered carrying the two flags of the combatant Irish forces, the tricolour of the National Volunteers and the plough-and-stars of the Irish Citizen Army. It happened that on the fourth night of the production there was present a large number of women closely associated with the 'men of 1916', those who had fought, died, or had been imprisoned. The sight of the flags sparked off massive resistance to what was perceived as an insult to the patriot dead. 'Women screamed and sang songs ... A red-haired damsel in the gallery removed her shoes and flung them heatedly into the mêlée beneath.' Then the fight began in earnest:

> Twenty women rushed from the pit to the stalls. Two of them succeeded in reaching the stage, where a general melee took place. The invading women were

thrown bodily back into the orchestra. A young man then tried to reach the stage, but was cut off by the lowering of the curtain. This he grabbed, swinging out on it in a frantic endeavour to pull it down. Women rushed to aid him in this project, but he was suddenly thrown into the stalls by a sharp blow from one of the actors. The pandemonium created a panic among a section of the audience, who dashed for the exits and added to the confusion.

As soon as the curtain was raised again, up dashed another youth to the stage and got into grips with two actresses opening the next scene. Immediately a couple of actors rushed from the wings and unceremoniously pushed off the intruder. Another man had got on the stage by this time and was attacked by a number of players. He retaliated vigorously, and after several blows were exchanged, a hardy punch on the jaw [by Barry Fitzgerald] hurled him into the stalls.

Meanwhile altercations were going on among the two sections of the audience. For several minutes the players calmly walked up and down the stage, but the performance was not resumed. A change came over the troubled scene when a party of detectives and uni-formed police arrived and quickly distributed them-selves through different parts of the house ... (Lowery, *Whirlwind*, pp. 30–31).

Yeats then came forward to address the audience. Now at the height of his powers and loaded with honours (the Nobel Prize had been awarded him in 1923), Yeats spoke with great authority. He was a Senator in the upper house of the Irish Free State government; he was chairman of the Abbey's Board of Directors and its managing director; he was not only the voice of the Abbey Theatre but virtually the voice of liberated Ireland. And what he had to say was to recall the days of Synge's reception over *The Playboy of the Western World* and to rebuke the present audience: 'You have disgraced yourselves again. Is this to be an ever-recurring celebration of the arrival of Irish genius? Once more you have rocked the cradle of genius.' O'Casey's reputation was established, he said, through this negative and violent response. 'This is his apotheosis.' (Lowery, p. 31).

O'Casey had to look up 'apotheosis' in his dictionary when he got home. To his surprise, he found that Yeats had placed him among the gods. Yet O'Casey knew all too well that to many people he was in the gutter, having betrayed the ideals of the 1916 Rising. As he left the theatre that night O'Casey was verbally abused by a group of nationalist women, who called him a traitor and a pro-Britain propagandist. ' "Yes," said one, leaning against the wall, "an' I'd like you to know that there isn't a prostitute in Ireland from one end of it to th' other." ' (*Inishfallen, Fare Thee Well*, pp. 176–7).

A public debate followed, first in the newspapers and then in a hall rented for the occasion on 1 March 1926. O'Casey's main opponent was Mrs Hannah Sheehy-Skeffington, a suffragette and widow of the pacifist shot by a British soldier during Easter Week, 1916. She was a woman of considerable presence, who spoke on behalf of all women involved in the 1916 Rising, and she had much support at the debate. Her main point was that *The Plough and the Stars* was 'a travesty of Easter Week, and that it concentrated on pettiness and squalor, unrelieved by a gleam of heroism' (Lowery, p. 100). O'Casey replied as best he could, saying he had not tried to write about 'heroes' and never would. Maud Gonne McBride, once Yeats's beloved, made the point that if O'Casey did not believe in heroes he should not have introduced a real one into his play in the form of Pádraic Pearse.

The issue was thus quite clear-cut: to the republicans and especially the women in that camp, *The Plough* was a disgraceful slur on those who had fought and died in 1916 and on that basis alone ought to be swept from the stage of the so-called national theatre. To O'Casey himself and his supporters, *The Plough* was great art and on this basis should be acclaimed, regardless of political considerations. Here was a play, however, where the art-versus-politics argument could never be resolved. *The Plough* is a political play; it is a modern history play. It is also a humanist play, in which characters and their fates appeal very strongly to audiences' feelings. The conflict between ideology and artistic achievement was and remains the major critical question surrounding *The Plough and the Stars*.

For O'Casey himself, the row over *The Plough* had lifelong implications. His *Juno and the Paycock* had been playing successfully in a London theatre since November 1925 and he was now invited over to supervise its transfer to a bigger theatre in March 1926. This would mark a major break with Dublin and the working-class conditions which had formed O'Casey as man and writer. He was aware what a big step it was, though at first he thought it would be temporary. He left Dublin on 5 March 1926 and was never again to return to live in Ireland. Thus *The Plough and the Stars*, which was to become an international success in due course, and the play most often revived at the Abbey Theatre, by its first reception brought to an end an important phase in

O'Casey's career. His next play, *The Silver Tassie* (1928), would be rejected by the Abbey and would cause another great controversy. O'Casey settled in England and never again wrote for the Abbey Theatre. Thereby he lost a workshop and a body of actors to write for and to collaborate with. His exile was, in a way, tragic.

Structure and Action

It should be obvious, having read the play, that *The Plough and the Stars* is not structured along conventional lines. There is no single plot as such. True, we join the young Clitheroe couple in the opening scenes and form the impression that the play will deal with their love and fortunes in the face of imminent political crisis. But Act Two puts paid to the idea of a well-made play which develops from an opening situation into a domestic crisis, then into complications with various threats to happiness, until the 'obligatory scene' is reached and the expected confrontation takes place which leaves only the dénouement of the plot to take place in the closing scene. As was made clear in the preceding chapters on *The Shadow of a Gunman* and *Juno and the Paycock*, O'Casey did not write in this way. But *The Plough and the Stars* is actually more extreme in its avoidance of conventional dramatic form than either of its two predecessors.

Act Two, in fact, is the key to the structure because, even though he avoided the form of the well-made play, O'Casey, as artist, had to provide the form which would best accommodate the content of his play. Act Two was originally a one-act play entitled *The Cooing of Doves*, submitted to the Abbey in the early 1920s and rejected. When he began to write *The Plough* in October 1924, then entitled *The Easter Lily Aflame*, what was in O'Casey's mind, he says, was that he had already written a play about the 'Black-and-Tan period' (1920) and a play about the Irish civil war (1922–3), 'but no play yet around the period of the actual Easter Rising, which was the beginning of all that happened afterward'. (Ayling, *Casebook*, p. 139) So that became his theme, and he allowed it to grow and combine in his mind with such symbols as the Irish flag, the tricolour, and the flag of the Irish Citizen Army, the plough-and-stars. 'I never make a scenario [plot outline], depending on the natural growth of a play rather than on any method of joinery.' (Ayling, *Casebook*, p. 140) He brings the two flags together in a public house, while outside the meeting takes place, corresponding to the actual meeting on 25 October 1915 which reconciled the Volunteers (under Pádraic Pearse) and the Irish Citizen Army (under James Connolly). In particular, the flag of the Irish Citizen Army, symbolising the workers ever aspiring to higher things, gave O'Casey his theme. 'It was this flag that fired in my mind the title for the play; and the events that swirled around the banner and that of the Irish Volunteers ... that gave me all the humour, pathos and dialogue that fill the play.' (Ayling, *Casebook*, p. 139) The structure thus grew from a central idea: the betrayal of the cause of Labour by the delusion of romantic patriotism. (This betrayal was even more clear when Labour failed to gain support in elections following the foundation of the Irish Free State in 1922.) Because of this thematic approach, the play does not suffer when Nora Clitheroe and her family problems are left out of Act Two. That act, O'Casey tells us, was filled largely by the rejected *The Cooing of Doves*: 'It went in with but a few minor changes.' (Ayling, *Casebook*, p. 140)

The key to Act Two, and thus the key to the structure of *The Plough* as a whole, lies in the juxtaposition of two totally contrasting worlds of experience. This is how O'Casey as playwright usually got his best effects. In this instance, the outside world of high-minded politics, articulated by the Figure in the Window, is violently brought into contact with the inside world of ordinary people satisfying basic human appetites. This collision releases a powerful delivery of irony. It is not that O'Casey mocks the speeches of the Figure in the Window: it is worth noting how the people in the pub often praise his words and respond with enthusiasm ('It's th' sacred thruth, mind you, what that man's afther sayin'' p. 183). The real point is that this enthusiasm is a form of intoxication, or, looked at the other way, the pub is a metaphor for the political response of the working class to idealistic rhetoric.

When the fighting begins in the pub, first between Mrs Gogan and Mrs Burgess and then between the Covey and Fluther, we have to see these battles as something of a parody of the great fight for freedom being eulogised by the Figure in the Window. Thus, the juxtaposition of high and low ideals is comic and provides the structural means for O'Casey to expose the dangerous inadequacy of the Figure's language and doctrine.

After Act Two the action returns to the domestic concerns of Nora Clitheroe and from this point to the end what we witness is tragic displacement. As the Rising breaks out and Nora goes in search of her husband Jack, the contrast is heightened between two sets of values, the domestic and the militaristic. The domestic values include fertility, the bringing of new life, as in Nora's pregnancy; the militaristic values include bloodshed, the destruction of life, as in Lieutenant Langan's wounds and the body that Nora describes, where 'every twist of his body was a cry against th' terrible thing that had happened to him' (p. 209). If we are reading the play adequately we will notice that Nora's pregnancy/fertility carries forward the motif of Mrs Gogan's baby in Act Two, embroiled in a battle that is there comic but deadly serious in Act Three. Nora's premature baby joins Mollser in the coffin in Act Four, underlining the waste and needlessness of such infant mortality.

O'Casey's way of organising the action, then, is to run several little plots at once, overlapping and repeating themes and motifs, and through these parallels and contrasts moving the main action along, which is the ill-fated attempt by Nora to keep her family together and to expand it.

In this pattern of repetitive action the use of space should be noticed. In complete defiance of the common description of his dramatic art as realistic, O'Casey increasingly used symbolism and other anti-realistic forms. The pub in Act Two and how it is combined with the exterior scene of the political meeting has already been commented on. The space onstage is in this way used in a style one would have to call *expressionistic*, that is, the Figure in the Window (who remains unnamed) looms up as if from a dream and invades the space of the public house with his voice and blurry presence. This is not realism, but a more experimental and more effective mode of staging the action. Fellow-playwright Denis Johnston, in an astute review of *The Plough* in 1926, said that as a realist O'Casey was 'an impostor': O'Casey's talent could not 'be bound by the four dismal walls of orthodox realism'. (Johnston, p. 85)

Act Three, indeed, transfers to the streets, and the space provides an image of people very much 'on the outside', powerless, removed from both the fight for freedom (which does not concern them) and from any share in the material wealth of society. When the Woman from Rathmines briefly enters this space we see vividly, if briefly, what a dead end, what a vacuum, it is: she desperately needs to escape to the safety of her middle-class suburb. By this time the looting has started, and the deprived people's need to steal in order to have a lifestyle equal to the middle class is vividly seen in Mrs Gogan and Mrs Burgess allying to bring home consumer goods of all kinds. A carnival spirit contrasts sharply with the back-ground of the Rising, and O'Casey's Elizabethan style of staging allows these two actions to go on at the same time without a change of scene: the entrance of the three soldiers, with Langan badly wounded, underlines the success of this staging method here.

Then Act Four brings us to Bessie Burgess's dingy flat at the top of the tenement. Here, the symbolism is all too apparent: the apartment has '*a look of compressed con-finement*' (p. 226). The space symbolises a trap, '*poverty bordering on destitution*'. It is the end of the line. Here Nora is displaced, out of her element, out of her home, and out of her mind. The setting allows this tragic stage of the action sharp definition. The coffin onstage in such a confined space, which the men use as a card-table, is a powerful image. It is waiting to be taken out; so too are the men; the surprise is that Bessie is also to be removed, dead, and the space finally occupied by the two British soldiers. The outside world of militarism thus finally invades and takes over the inside world of domestic safety, and the action is complete. The setting, the staging, the image of the soldiers sitting to drink the tea Nora made for Jack and their joining in the song outside, provide a masterly unification of theme and action. We see here, if we haven't seen it already, how O'Casey weaves together the various strands of the action so that there is finally created a devastating and ironic effect. This converging on the final image of the fire within, the fire without, the song without matched by the song within, concentrates the viewer's or reader's response in such a way that she or he is moved by the tragic destruction, the pincer movement of events, which has befallen the helpless residents of this symbolic tenement house.

Characters and Themes

By the time he came to write *The Plough and the Stars* O'Casey well understood the primacy of characterisation in drama. This is not to deny the importance of 'action', but it is to declare quite emphatically that O'Casey's plays are *not* plot-driven but character-driven. Technically, what O'Casey does breaks the rules of good dramaturgy – a playwright isn't supposed to introduce a character once only and never even have her mentioned by another character: witness Rosie Redmond, seen only in Act Two. A more glaring example is the unnamed Woman from Rathmines, who has no more than one page of text in Act Three and is never seen or heard of again. Even O'Casey himself, a stout defender of his experimental style, later condemned this episode. The Woman, he wrote in *The Green Crow* (1956), 'had neither rhyme nor reason for being there; a character that was in every way a false introduction; one who could have no conceivable connection with any of the others from the play's beginning to the play's end' (p. 9). But this character is not usually omitted in production because, like Rosie Redmond, she throws light on the realities of Irish life in the period in which *The Plough* is set. The Woman from Rathmines is an extreme case, but her inclusion indicates how O'Casey understood characterisation. In general, his characters exist to *show* something rather than to do something: we *see* what they stand for, not in the sense that we see immediately that Rosie Redmond is a prostitute but in the sense that she is dependent on men, that she is exploited by her landlord, that she is one of the defenceless whom the Rising will ignore and fail to help.

Characters in O'Casey do not do much; they are not agents of action in the conventional dramatic sense. Like characters in Dickens's novels or in some comic parts of Shakespeare's history plays (because O'Casey's Dublin plays are really history plays), O'Casey's characters are on the margins of great events rather than in the thick of them. What we see is how they cope with their power-lessness. Usually, they cope by inventing and sustaining eccentricities of manner and speech which force others in the community to beware and to make space for them. Once given that space – and a character like Peter Flynn is perpetually complaining that he is *not* given this space – an O'Casey character will settle into a performance of the invented role rather than actually do anything which changes the situation. There are exceptions to this generalisation, notably Minnie Powell in *The Shadow of a Gunman* and Juno Boyle in *Juno and the Paycock*, but such exceptions prove the rule: 'character' in the sense of 'hero' is, as Mrs Madigan might say in *Juno and the Paycock*, 'null and void'.

Therefore, in *The Plough and the Stars* for the most

part one has characters who jostle for the space in which to perform the role that brings each of them compensation for loss of social and economic status. Thus Mrs Gogan, for example, whose voice is the first one we hear in the play, is a widow with many children to support, one of whom is the dying Mollser and another a baby, and yet Mrs Gogan is a curious, busy-body type who takes pleasure in the spectacle of death. There is, of course, something comical about this macabre side of Mrs Gogan, but the point to be made is *her need to avoid the realities of her own economic position*. She invents things: she decides that the delivery of Nora's hat is a sign of Nora's snobbery. But we soon learn that the hat is a present from Jack and so is not a sign of Nora's self-indulgence at all. When it comes to Mollser's consumption, because there is nothing she can do for her, Mrs Gogan prefers to believe Mollser is getting better. When she is told at one point that Mollser 'looks as if she was goin' to faint', she is quick to snap back, 'She's never any other way but faintin'!' (p. 218). Mrs Gogan fights with Bessie Burgess for the perambulator only to use it for looting: this is the only action she takes and it is a significant one. Rising or no Rising, she has to feed and clothe her family and will steal to do so. She is finally 'in her element' when Mollser dies, as Fluther notes: 'mixin' earth to earth, an' ashes t'ashes an' dust to dust, an' revellin' in plumes an' hearses, last days an' judgements!' (p. 235). This 'performance' element is a part of her character.

It is also a part of the characters of Uncle Peter and the Covey. Each of these is a caricature or two-dimensional type, exaggerated for amusement. Each exists mainly – like characters out of Dickens – to maintain endlessly the provocative and/or irritable responses they show from the very outset. One would have to say, however, that the Covey, for all that he *is* a caricature of a swaggering know-all, is to some extent O'Casey's spokesman on the political meaning of the play. One can instance three occasions where this is so:

(1) In Act One the Covey accuses the Irish Citizen Army of bringing disgrace to the flag, the plough-and-stars, because it was a Labour flag and ought not to be associated with a middle-class nationalist revolution such as the Volunteers were planning.

(2) When the Figure in the Window (Act Two) praises war as a glorious thing, which had already brought 'heroism' back to Europe in World War I and which must be welcomed in Ireland as the 'Angel of God', the Covey dismisses this idea as mere 'dope' (p. 191). He goes on to repeat this charge to Fluther (p. 196), and a row develops. Whereas the Covey is a troublemaker, and is satirised as a socialist fanatic, O'Casey actually shared the Covey's belief about Pearse's speech. Therefore, the Covey is useful in the play as a counterblast to Pearse's romantic nationalism.

(3) In the last act, when the Covey preaches to the English soldier about the evils of consumption arising from the capitalist system, Corporal Stoddart concedes the point and adds that he is a socialist himself but has to do his duty as a soldier nevertheless. The Covey argues that the *only* duty of a socialist is the emancipation of the workers, and when Stoddart replies that one has to fight for his country just the same we get the telling question from the Covey: 'You're not fightin' for your counthry here, are you?' (p. 236), thus pointing up the false analysis made by this confused Englishman, whose nationalism,

like the nationalism of the Irish Volunteers, has taken precedence over socialism and has left problems like consumption unsolved.

The Covey is therefore responsible for injecting into the play the major *agon* or debating point on which the tragedy depends, for O'Casey's own analysis was that the 1916 Rising was a mistake so far as the Dublin working class was concerned. The Clitheroes, standing for that class, are destroyed because of the nationalism to which Jack Clitheroe gives service (and his life). It is ironic that the irritating Covey, who is an armchair socialist and a bore, should nevertheless be the one to point up the flaw in the ideology driving the combatants.

O'Casey's representation of Jack Clitheroe differs from his more detailed characterisation of Nora, Fluther and Bessie, the three main characters in *The Plough*. It is obvious from the outset that Clitheroe's involvement in the fight for freedom is governed more by personal vanity than by political principle; both Mrs Gogan and Nora herself comment on his vanity. When Clitheroe switches from amorous stay-at-home to stern authoritarian in Act One it is only because his promotion in the Irish Citizen Army was kept secret by Nora. When he enters in Act Three in the midst of the Rising, the first thing Clitheroe says to Nora is that he wishes he had never left her (p. 219). Just as Bernard Shaw revealed the harsh realities of battle through the professional soldier Bluntschli in *Arms and the Man* (1894), so O'Casey exposes the frightening realities of revolution through the experience of Clitheroe. To this extent O'Casey's theme and purpose are pacifist. He brings out this theme much more fully in his characterisation of Nora. Meanwhile, Clitheroe is shown caught up in a romantic battle fuelled first by fanaticism and then by fear. His character disappears under the rubble of the Imperial Hotel, whose destruction Brennan graphically describes in Act Four. Brennan tries to transform Clitheroe's terrible death into a heroic end, but as Bessie Burgess points out Clitheroe was simply abandoned in a burning building (p. 230). O'Casey's insistence on stripping Clitheroe of heroic status is a major part of his pacifist theme.

Nora Clitheroe is presented in a more complex way than Jack or any of the minor characters. In the best drama, characters are both admirable and the opposite; at times we sympathise and at other times we are repelled. On the one hand Nora is clearly ambitious, a woman with drive and energy who is determined to get out of the tenements as soon as she can build up the means: hence the two lodgers in a small apartment. She has aspiration to middle-class status: she talks much of 'respectability' in Act One as among her primary aims for the household. All of this angers Bessie Burgess and fills Mrs Gogan with contempt (' "Many a good one", says I, "was reared in a tenement house",' p. 154). Nora expresses one of the major themes in the play when she emphasises the importance of the home and the need both to protect it and help it to prosper. As the play opens Nora is employing Fluther to fix a lock on her door – a move which Bessie sees as an insult to her personally – and this is symbolic. Nora needs to shut out trouble from the home. Mollser admires Nora's abilities as home-maker and wonders if she herself will ever be strong enough 'to be keepin' a home together for a man' (p. 179). This purpose might strike us today as somewhat sexist but the representation of women as nurturers and home-makers is crucial to O'Casey's mode of thinking. It is a premise or a given of this play, in particular, that masculine and feminine values are sharply differentiated: war and destruction of life are here destructive of the home, fertility and new life.

Nora in this regard has a symbolic function. She stands for everything that is not death-bringing and is life-preserving. In Act Three we see clearly Nora's hatred of war as the agent of destruction of domestic life. Her passion makes her see only the fear and 'cowardice' of the combatants, 'afraid to say they're afraid' (p. 209). The women who opposed *The Plough* and who rioted on the fourth night saw Nora as the enemy, the spokesperson for O'Casey's anti-republicanism. But O'Casey deliberately allows Nora to become hysterical and to become excessive in her feelings against the Rising: this is *her* character, not O'Casey's propaganda. And he allows Mrs Gogan – of all people – to counter Nora's charge of the men's cowardice: 'Oh, they're not cowards anyway' (p. 209). We sympathise with Nora but we feel she goes 'over the top' in her reaction. Similarly, in Act Four, we are mainly sympathetic towards Nora in her broken state but we see, too, that she causes the death of Bessie Burgess. Nora's weakness creates tragic conflict, and this weakness is all that some critics, such as William Irwin Thompson, see: 'Nora is armed with little more than tears and imploring tugs at the sleeve ... [and] is only an object of pity' by the end, for 'it is difficult to make a tragic heroine out of a pretty girl' (p. 162). But surely this view is far more sexist than anything O'Casey presented in 1926? Why should not 'a pretty girl' (and Nora is in fact a married *woman*!) be a tragic heroine? Is Juliet not a tragic heroine in Shakespeare's play? Nora chooses to chase out after Jack in the battle, which causes the miscarriage which in turn loses her her sanity; her best efforts fail to save Jack and that scenario is tragic by any definition. What we must conclude – apart from the fact that critics can be woefully wrong – is that Nora is at times aggravating and at times entirely sympathetic. Her humanity resides in this contradiction, and makes her all the more impressive as a dramatic creation.

The critic Ronald Ayling refers to O'Casey's skill in 'distancing' his major characters and this is what we find with Nora, Fluther and Bessie. They are not allowed to win our unqualified approval. On the contrary, for much of the play Fluther and Bessie are presented negatively. From the start Fluther is the common man: friendly, tolerant, amusing, but with a weakness for strong liquor. One of the first London critics of *The Plough*, James Agate, referred to Fluther as 'Falstaffian', and the description has stuck because of its aptness. Shakespeare's Falstaff is larger than life, robust, irresponsible, fond of drinking, Lord of Misrule, and not only witty in himself but the cause of wit in others. Fluther shows in Act Two how Falstaffian he can be, and is rewarded with Rosie Redmond's company as he leaves the pub. In the argument with the Covey, Fluther may not show intellectual superiority but he wins our hearts through his sheer unwillingness to be overcome by scientific jargon. In Act Three his Falstaffian nature is plainly on view when, ignoring the glorious cause which set his blood boiling in Act Two, he returns stone drunk from looting and cries out his defiance and indifference: 'Th' whole city can topple home to hell, for Fluther!' (p. 224). Finally, he fails Nora in her hour of need when he is incapable of going to fetch a doctor. He is thus anything but a hero; he is more the comic braggart thrown into a tragic situation. Thus we are 'distanced' and forced to see Fluther's faults alongside his attractions.

This 'distancing' method is combined with what Ronald Ayling calls O'Casey's 'balancing' of the dramatic action. There is no dominating character in *The Plough*, because O'Casey wanted always to present the group, the community, as the dramatic focus. Individual characters dominate for a scene or so and 'are then firmly distanced before they can disrupt the balance of the whole' (Ayling, p. 178). Thus Fluther – like Nora – is at times admired (for example, when he brings Nora safely home), and at other times blamed (as when he is too drunk to help further). In Act Four we see Fluther standing up bravely to the aggressive Sergeant (p. 241), and here the better side of his character is again on view. Yet this is the same Fluther who swallows down his looted whiskey as if there were no tomorrow: 'If I'm goin' to be whipped away, let me be whipped away when it's empty, an' not when it's half full!' (p. 229). Against that amusing self-indulgence we must place Mrs Gogan's tribute to Fluther's help with the funeral arrangement for Mollser (p. 237). He is thus a tissue of contradictory qualities, and in a strange way these contradictions make him seem more rather than less convincing.

Bessie Burgess is the greatest example of O'Casey's skill in characterisation in *The Plough*. Introduced as a termagant, Bessie is provided with a history which renders her political attitude as meaningful as her social aggression: she is presumably widowed – no Mr Burgess is ever mentioned, and from her rebuke to Mrs Gogan in Act Two about 'weddin' lines' (p. 192) it is likely there *was* a Mr Burgess – and she has a son fighting the Germans in Flanders and about to return home with a shattered arm (p. 238). Bessie stands out, then, as a loyalist, a Protestant unionist, in a community predominantly Roman Catholic and separatist. Her courage marks her out when she opposes the Easter Rising by flaunting the Union Jack from her window and singing 'Rule, Britannia' at the top of her voice (p. 208).

But courage aside, there is a marvellous wholeness about Bessie Burgess, a mixture of hostility and generosity, aggression and tenderness, cruelty and uncommon kindness. She confronts Nora for her air of superiority in Act One and Mrs Gogan for her breach of decorum in bringing a baby into a public bar among men. She is a fighter, literally in Act Two, verbally in Act Three (over the pram), and at most other times. But with Mollser she is kind and gentle: '*she gives a mug of milk to Mollser silently*' (p. 210). The 'silently' is typical. When Nora is in trouble towards the end of Act Three it is Bessie who first goes outside and carries her in, and then risks life and limb to go for a doctor in spite of her personal dislike of Nora – actions speak louder than words.

And, of course, in Act Four we see the extent of Bessie's charity and generosity when she mothers, nurses and protects the damaged Nora in her own cramped apartment. Bessie is killed trying to preserve Nora's life, and the Christian strength of her action is by no means undermined when Bessie reverts to her earlier scorn for Nora as she realises she has been shot on her account. Her use of the word 'bitch' here (p. 244) was rightly defended by Yeats as 'necessary' when the unofficial censor tried to remove it from the script: 'the scene is magnificent and we are loth to alter a word of it' (Lady Gregory, *Journals*). The word was retained. It is part of the proof that O'Casey's representation of Bessie was *not* sentimental but realistic.

In his portrayal of Bessie, then, O'Casey is careful once again to ensure that she remains ambivalent. As Ayling justly remarks (p. 186), 'we neither admire nor despise her indiscriminately, for her heroic stature is enhanced, though never exaggerated, by seeing her character in perspective.'

The ambivalences and contradictions O'Casey introduces into his characterisation in *The Plough* provide just the sort of distancing which allows the reader/spectator to see the play *critically* and to appreciate what Jack Lindsay (p. 193) calls its 'full dialectics' – that is, how the clashing ideologies within this society are seen in their irreconcilable conflict.

Language

The point has been made in the earlier chapters on *The Shadow of a Gunman* and *Juno and the Paycock* that O'Casey's language records and elaborates Dublin speech. The reader is advised to read those sections now, for this is also the case in *The Plough*.

The Plough exhibits a richness of speech in two quite different ways. One is through expansion of a statement for special effect beyond what is strictly necessary. An example is Nora's heated response in Act One to Jack's sexual advances: 'It's hard for a body to be always keepin' her mind bent on makin' thoughts that'll be no longer than th' length of your own satisfaction' (p. 173). This is a rather poetic way of saying, 'It's hard to say the right thing,' but Nora's way of putting it neatly turns realism aside in favour of alliteration (*m*ind ... *m*akin' ... *l*onger than th' *l*ength' ...) and euphemism ('sexual satisfaction'). Another example is Fluther's advice to Mrs Gogan in Act

Two to ignore Bessie Burgess: 'Th' safest way to hindher her from havin' any enjoyment out of her spite, is *to dip our thoughts into the fact of her bein' a female person* that has moved out of th' sight of ordinary sensible people' (p. 190, emphasis added). This simply means, 'It's best to ignore her completely', but the beauty of the speech lies in the adept cultivation of more words than are strictly necessary. Looked at more closely, Fluther's speech uses a powerful metaphor ('to dip our thoughts'), but the metaphor keeps sliding into clauses that seem, but refuse, to clarify it ('the fact of her bein' a female person that . . .'). It is rhetoric which delights through its ornateness.

The language used in the play is often hyperbolic in this way: it uses excess for effect. Uncle Peter's language is piled high with unnecessary words which nevertheless provide a wonderful rhythm and sense of exaggeration: 'I'll leave you to th' day when th' all-pitiful, all-merciful, all-lovin' God 'll be handin' you to th' angels to be rievin' an' roastin' you, tearin' an' tormentin' you, burnin' an' blastin' you!' (p. 163). The sentence builds up to the word 'God', and seems a patient prayer, but then it turns around and calls for the 'angels', when Peter secretly means 'demons', to torture the Covey without mercy. The whole speech is a comic about-turn which reveals the vindictiveness of the hypocritical Peter. His use of alliteration within phrases coupling verbs of destruction (*t*earin' and *t*ormentin', etc.) provides delight to the audience.

Peter is not alone in being gifted with this ornate language. Virtually all of the characters within the tenements use this energetic speech as if it were their main resource in an economy which deprives them of real power. Peter curses eloquently simply because he can take no action. Language *is* power to these characters. Its power is sometimes comic, as when Fluther remarks, 'when you'd look at him [Peter], you'd wondher whether th' man was makin' fun o' th' costume, or th' costume was makin' fun o' th' man!' (p. 189). But the language is usually aggressive as well as comic. Indeed, the language is most often funny *because* the purpose is aggressive: these characters are nearly always verbally sparring, because they can't usefully engage in any action.

There is a second type of speech in *The Plough* and that is the more carefully constructed long speech. Here O'Casey was probably influenced by the use of the 'set speech' in Shakespeare. Because O'Casey's characters greatly admire language and frequently use it expertly to put down or displace others, it follows that they also admire a good speech themselves. This is part of the Irish tradition, found also, for example, in Synge's *The Playboy of the Western World*. Thus when the Figure in the Window begins his address – 'It is a glorious thing to see arms in the hands of Irishmen' (p. 182) – the response in the pub is immediate. Rosie describes the words as 'sacred thruth'; the Barman says if he was a little younger they would send him 'plungin' mad into th' middle of it!' (p. 183). Peter and Fluther are physically affected by the rhetoric, intoxicated by it even before they touch a drop of whiskey. Fluther describes the speeches as pattering on the people's heads like rain falling on corn, generative, stirring and productive. In short, the political rhetoric is *moving*. O'Casey lets these speeches from the Figure in the Window (all four of them) have their own effect: he does not put them into dialect spelling, and he does not suggest that they are in any way ironic. He allows them their formality, their high style, and he allows them their powerful effect.

This effect culminates in the strange, incantatory, religious language of the three soldiers who enter with the flags towards the end of Act Two. Having heard the Figure's speeches outside, they are stirred to die for Ireland. They agree that Ireland is greater than a mother and greater than a wife. Hearing now the final speech, an excerpt from Pádraic Pearse's oration over the grave of the Fenian hero O'Donovan Rossa, the three soldiers are in a state not just of fanaticism but of dangerous ecstasy as they pledge themselves to die for the independence of Ireland: 'So help us God!' (p. 201). The point is that the political rhetoric has aroused political madness. O'Casey establishes this point through equating language with intoxicating liquor. Nora's anti-war speeches in Act Three should be looked at as rhetoric answering the speeches of the Figure in the Window.

A different example of the longer speech is seen in the 'flyting match' in Act Three between Mrs Gogan and Bessie Burgess. A flyting match was a medieval debate which could become violent. We have a good example when Mrs Gogan and Bessie argue over who has more right to appropriate the pram (for the purposes of looting). Consider Mrs Gogan's speech which begins: 'That remark of yours, Mrs Bessie Burgess' (p. 214); the point she has to make is that the pram was left in her care. Mrs Burgess retaliates with the point that Mrs Gogan's complaints about the pram as an obstruction disqualify any claim she has to its use. Both speeches are metaphysical: they are plainly empty rhetoric. It is like the jargon used by negotiators in an industrial dispute: language as smokescreen for self-interest. The fact that the two women form an alliance and go out sharing the pram underlines the power of language once again. Each woman may have been speaking nonsense but having failed, like wrestlers, to gain a knockout, they agree on a draw and share the spoils. O'Casey uses this farcical moment to draw out the comic side of difference. In a parody of the alliance between the Volunteers and the Irish Citizen Army he shows how practical self-interest with a material end in view is far more meaningful to the deprived classes than theoretical debate. Language as a form of looting is gleefully celebrated.

A final and different example is what in classical drama is called the 'Nuntius's speech'. Towards the end of a tragedy a messenger usually enters to announce what has happened to Oedipus or Agamemnon or whoever, inside the palace. A long speech is delivered, full of details calculated to stir the hearts of the audience and prepare them for the final speeches of lament from the chorus. In Shakespeare's plays the messenger's speeches are shorter because violence has already been seen onstage (the description of Ophelia's death in *Hamlet* might be an exception). In all three of his Dublin plays, O'Casey makes use of the ancient Greek convention of a Nuntius who relates solemnly how one of the main characters – Minnie Powell, Johnny Boyle, Jack Clitheroe – met her or his death. In Act Four of *The Plough* Brennan describes the so-called noble end of Jack Clitheroe in language stuffed with conventional platitudes. O'Casey here insists on puncturing the description by having Bessie pour scorn on Brennan's own cowardice, and yet the conventional picture remains to contrast with Nora's demented state. Mrs Gogan has two such formal speeches in Act Four (pp. 237, 246).

It is worth noting here that language is shown up as finally inadequate; the play ends in stalemate. The song that the British soldiers sing merely repeats what the Figure in the Window called for: men to leave hearth and home to fight for their country. The major irony – and all of O'Casey's tragicomedies end ironically – is that the 'home fires' *are* burning now in Dublin, but burning in destruction and not in domestic security. Because of the Ireland–England divide, the language held in common finally breaks down over the meaning of 'home', the very thing Nora Clitheroe cared most about. Her mad speeches show how dislocated she, as representative Irish woman, now is after the Rising. Her delusion that she is at home waiting for Jack is presented as something non-verbal: Brennan is told to *look* at her, to 'see' the way she is (pp. 232, 234), and how incapable she is of being *told*, of being given the truth in words. The image of Dublin burning thus challenges language and confronts the audience with the tragic irony of 'keeping the home fires burning'.

Performance

The Plough and the Stars is the most frequently staged of O'Casey's plays and therefore his most successful in performance. It should be remembered that the disturbances at the Abbey in 1926 happened only on the fourth night of the first production; although the play was controversial, it was popular. Productions in London (1926) and New York (1927) were equally well received by the critics, although always, from those premières down to revivals in the 1980s and 1990s, there have been critics who see the play as scrappy, melodramatic and lacking in clarity of theme. Of course, it is the task of the director to bring out the coherence and clarity of the play onstage.

The worst kind of production presents *The Plough* as

an aimless entertainment, as if the characters exist in a television situation-comedy where there happen to be militaristic noises offstage. But the key to watching or reading *The Plough* lies in the progressively intense *rhythm of events*. Every play has a rhythm. It may seem merely to 'unroll' in a series of haphazard and varied events, but if it is well written it will organise these events in a design which accumulates like a dynamic jigsaw. It has to be dynamic, because the design cannot be merely pictorial. What happens onstage (which in reading we must try to visualise) is as much like an extended piece of music as it is a picture being completed. As in music, there are slow parts and quick parts, sudden shifts from soft to loud notes, chords which sound themes which will repeat again and again, and a constant beat which holds the whole piece together as it moves towards a climax. In reading *The Plough* we must discover this rhythm. It may help to study the way Act Four brings to a harsh closure many of the themes sounded in Act One. If the reader looks closely at Act Four they will notice that the *mood* is now very different from Act One. In contrast to the lively spirits, the energy of teasing, abuse and delightful sense of life, Act Four is sombre, tense, watchful, the characters constantly having to subdue outbreaks of dispute lest Nora's rest be disrupted, while the presence of the coffin onstage sets the tone for a disturbing sense of death.

A useful way to study this rhythm is to break down an act into micro-units, or what in American theatre are called 'beats'. A beat is a scene within a scene just long enough to contain its own energy. Each beat has its own purpose. For example, in Act Four the first beat is concerned with the card game. While the three men play cards, they discuss what happened to Nora: the game provides a focus for concentration. This is far better than if the three men simply sat around talking. The *ritual* of card-playing paves the way for Nora's ritual of making tea: these normal activities actually increase our sense here of abnormality. The card game, as such, does not matter. Far more important are Mollser's death, Nora's loss of her baby, and Nora's breakdown. By means of the ritualistic card game, then, O'Casey supplies a chorus on the tragic action.

In the next 'beat' Bessie enters to silence the men arguing over the cards. This little scene conveys a sense of urgency and anxiety. We see Bessie in a new light – that of nurse and protector. A third beat follows with the entrance of Brennan, who is looking for Nora. His purpose gives a tension to this little scene: he has a message to deliver. The need of the others to protect Nora from any further bad news means an intensification here of the atmosphere of anxiety generated by the opening of Act Four, with its very important stage-directions.

The rhythm is thus building up moment by moment, tightening the screws, so to speak, until the British soldiers enter. Brennan's presence is a threat to the safety of the other three men. The fourth beat, however, comes with Nora's entrance just after Brennan's account of Clitheroe's death and his sentimental assurance that Nora will be proud when she knows 'she has had a hero for a husband' (p. 231). Bessie corrects this view with the declaration that a sight of Nora would disprove any such idea, and it is at just this moment that Nora enters. The purpose, then, is for Nora *visually* to offset Brennan's prediction and in that way to get the audience to sweep away all militaristic propaganda and to invest feeling instead in Nora's victimage, Nora's representative status as tragic sacrifice.

Some critics have thought the echo of Shakespeare's Ophelia in her mad scene too obvious here, too much of a distraction. But this is not, or ought not to be, so. Madness on stage *is* a visual matter: it is 'ostension' or showing in iconic form the alienated state of a pathetic figure. When, in this fourth beat, Bessie remarks, 'isn't this pitiful!' (p. 232) the audience's response is being carefully directed. Fluther points out to Brennan what Nora's derangement signifies: 'Now *you can see* th' way she is, man' (p. 232, emphasis added). The Covey repeats this formulation after Bessie leads Nora off again: 'Now *that you've seen* how bad she is . . .' (p. 234). The audience has seen the same thing, and so is actively implicated. A good play will involve the spectators in just this way, the performances on stage combining with this visualisation. They form an ensemble or group concentrating on the deepening mood.

The fifth, brief, beat records Brennan easing himself for protection into the circle of the three card-players. This is followed by the sixth beat when Corporal Stoddart enters. Here the mood shifts abruptly to danger; his purpose is to get the coffin out and do a surveillance of the occupants of the apartment. He is led by the Covey into a discussion of socialism and child mortality versus the perils of warfare. The one detail revealed in this scene is that the Rising is nearly over and was never more than a dog-fight (p. 236). The sound-effects of a sniper's bullet and the eerie cry of 'Ambulance!' immediately throw the Corporal's summary into ironic question. He resolves to find the sniper, and the tension is given another heightening twist. The seventh beat comes with Mrs Gogan's arrival to supervise the removal of the coffin, and here the mood expands to arouse sympathy for her and admiration for Fluther. The beats which follow relate to Bessie's angry assertion of her Protestant identity to Corporal Stoddart, Peter's old irritation over the Covey's teasing, and Fluther's comic acceptance of incarceration in a church so long as the men may play cards.

All of this unrolling action has to be seen as the careful dramatisation of a closing in, a closing down on the people. A constant sense of unease is maintained. In the ninth beat, after the sniper has struck again and Sergeant Tinley has entered in anger, the men are roughly evacuated in a mood of defiance, paving the way for Bessie and Nora's last scene. As before, Bessie is asleep when Nora enters, except that now a street battle is raging offstage and the sense of danger is acute. Bessie's wrestling with Nora results in Bessie being shot directly in front of the window that is upstage-centre, theatrically a commanding position. When the Abbey actress Marie Kean played the next, twelfth, beat in the 1966 television production of *The Plough* she made Bessie's death-scene remarkably moving. This is the only death actually witnessed in the course of a play where many die offstage; therefore, the performance of Bessie's death (as representative and as, again, something *seen*) is crucial to the effect of the ending. Marie Kean prolonged the death-scene (rather as Laurence Olivier prolonged the death of Richard III) so that her every movement, her twisting and crawling, communicated agony and desperation. The audience could not but feel both pity and terror here, as tragedy demands. The death of Bessie marks the absurd and yet the one truly heroic moment in this anti-heroic play, and caused O'Casey much trouble in the writing. Thus its performance is a matter of considerable importance if the effect is to be properly cathartic.

This scene is followed by two more beats, as Mrs Gogan escorts Nora away to her flat and the two British soldiers re-enter. As at the end of *Juno and the Paycock*, the effect of the final scene is ironic. O'Casey calls for a lighting effect: a '*glare in the sky*' seen through the back window flaring '*into a fuller and a deeper red*' (p. 246). In his notes for the lighting written for the Samuel French acting edition of *The Plough* in 1932, O'Casey explains what is needed: 'Two special red floods on illuminated cloth at window, back; these to be on dimmers, so that red glow rises and falls during Act, to indicate fires in city' (p. 71). The sudden flare into a fuller and deeper red signifies, as Sergeant Tinley says (p. 247), the British attack on the General Post Office, where Pearse, Connolly and the Irish forces are mainly stationed. The game is up. The final song, in which the two soldiers onstage join, is both an encouragement to this fire of retaliation and a celebration of cheerfulness very much at odds with all that has befallen the tenement dwellers.

The whole of Act Four, then, has relentlessly progressed towards this ironic interrogation of a victory for one side which is also a massive defeat for the other. In performance, the final moments are searingly moving and dismaying. Through that complex ending the audience, and the readers of the text, come to *see* (that word is again crucial) and thus register the folly and the horror of war.

Textual Notes

153 Maggie – elsewhere Mrs Gogan's first name is given as Jenny and Cissie.

154 derogatory – critical, ascribing blame. But Fluther uses the word to suit all occasions.

155 foostherin' – bustling about fussily (Dolan,
   Dictionary of Hiberno-English).

156 canonicals – clerical dress. Presumably Mrs Gogan
   means 'regimentals' or military dress.

  – Citizen Army – the Irish Citizen Army was founded
   by Jim Larkin in November 1913 as a defence force
   for the Dublin workers during the great lock-out of
   1913–14. O'Casey was the secretary for a time.

  – Liberty Hall – headquarters of the Irish Transport
   and General Workers' Union and of the Irish
   Citizen Army, located in Beresford Place.

  – figaries – Mrs Gogan possibly means 'filigree',
   ornamental work. 'Figary' (Hiberno-English) could
   mean 'stylish clothing' (Dolan, *Dictionary of
   Hiberno-English*).

159 Covey – a smart alec, a know-all person (Ayling,
   Seven Plays, glossary).

  – Plough an' th' Stars – the banner of the Irish Citizen
   Army.
   in seculo seculorum – for all eternity.

160 cunundhrums – conundrums, riddles. Here and
   throughout (compare 'mollycewels' for 'molecules'
   or 'wurum' for 'worm') O'Casey renders Dublin
   speech phonetically.

162 Georgina: The Sleepin' Vennis – *The Sleeping Venus*
   by Giorgione, sixteenth-century Italian painter.

164 Dear harp o' me counthry – one of the popular
   melodies of the Irish poet and songwriter Thomas
   Moore (1779–1852).

165 where your bowsey battlin' 'ill meet, maybe, with
   an encore – where your drunken fighting may be
   welcome. (Note the theatrical term 'encore'.)

166 Jenersky's *Thesis* – a fictional Marxist text.

- whole – complete. The phrase is Dublinese, 'a great fellow'.
- a glass o' malt – whiskey.

167 to speak proud things, an' lookin' like a mighty one – a possible quotation from the Bible, untraced.

168 g'up ower o' that – go away. Nora's rather refined speech here lapses into colloquialism (the phrase is spoken as one word); ower – 'out'.
- sorra – no (Hiberno-English, emphatic negative).

169 *the Foresters* – according to O'Casey, 'The Irish National Foresters is merely a benevolent Society, and those who wear the costume worn by Peter are a subject of amusement to intelligent Irishmen' (French's acting edition, 1932, p. 80).

171 Oh, where's th' slave so lowly – another of Moore's *Irish Melodies*, 1807.
varmint – vermin (Ayling, *Seven Plays*, glossary).

178 *The Soldiers' Song* – by Peadar Kearney (1883–1942), first published in 1912, later the Irish national anthem.

180 yous'll not escape from th' arrow that flieth be night – quotation from the Bible, Psalms 91: 5.
- titther – tittle, particle.

182 Curse o' God on th' haporth – Dublin slang for 'nothing at all'; 'haporth' – halfpenny-worth.
- It is a glorious thing ... of them! – lines taken from 'The Coming Revolution' (1913), a speech by Pádraic Pearse (1879–1916), leader of the Irish Volunteers.

183 gems – possibly 'gentlemen' (ironic).
- dhrink Loch Erinn dhry – colloquial expression for great thirst; presumably referring to Lough Erne in Co. Fermanagh.

- Wolfe Tone – Theobald Wolfe Tone (1763–98),
  founder of the United Irishmen, whose grave in
  Bodenstown, Co. Kildare, became a shrine for
  republicans from the centenary of Tone's death in
  1898. See also the note to p. 188.
  vice versa – the opposite way.

184 comrade soldiers ... country – lines from 'Peace and
  the Gael' (1915), a speech by Pádraic Pearse. The
  next sentence in the speech here is O'Casey's
  addition. It may be noted that Pearse's speech was
  delivered in *December* 1915, one month after
  O'Casey's specified time for Act Two.

187 shinannickin' afther Judies – chasing girls. The
  word 'shenanigans', or 'shinannickin', is usually a
  noun meaning, colloquially, 'mischievous behaviour,
  trickery' (Dolan, *Dictionary of Hiberno-English*).

188 Bodenstown – site of cemetery in Co. Kildare where
  the grave of Theobald Wolfe Tone is located (see
  note to p. 183).

189 little Catholic Belgium – the point here is that Bessie
  is a staunch Protestant with a son fighting in France.

190 flappers – flighty society girls.

- a woman that is loud an' stubborn ... house – a
  qotation from the Bible, Proverbs 7: 11. The
  reference is to a 'harlot' or whore.

- Cissie Gogan – compare 'Maggie' (p. 153) and
  'Jenny' (p. 192).

191 The last sixteen months ... God! – a second
  quotation from Pádraic Pearse's speech 'Peace and
  the Gael' (1915).

- Saint Vincent de Paul man – a charitable
  organisation which gives vouchers to the poor for
  food and clothing.

192 precept upon precept ... little – a quotation from
the Bible, Isaiah 28: 10. The passage is an attack on
drunkards.

– weddin' lines – marriage certificate (Ayling, *Seven
Plays*, glossary).

– Jinnie Gogan – earlier (p. 190), Mrs Gogan gave her
first name as Cissie and at the outset (p. 153) as
'Maggie'. O'Casey was not usually careless over
such details.

193 dawny – frail.

194 gom – a silly, a foolish person (Dolan, *Dictionary of
Hiberno-English*).

196 chiselur – child (usually spelt 'chiseller', Dublin
slang).

– Shan Van Vok – Fluther's rendering of the Gaelic,
Sean Bhean Bhocht, or 'poor old woman', i.e.,
Ireland.

199 bowsey – a disreputable drunkard; Dublin slang,
perhaps related to 'booze' (Dolan, *Dictionary of
Hiberno-English*)

200 malignified – Fluther means 'maligned', insulted.

– clatther – blow (Hiberno-English).

201 Our foes are strong ... peace! – from Pádraic
Pearse's 'O'Donovan Rossa – Graveside Oration'
(1915).

202 I once had a lover ... th' bed! – Rosie's song was
cut from the first production in 1926 at the horrified
insistence of the government representative on the
Abbey Board.

204 put much pass on – take much notice of.

– aself – itself, i.e. 'even'.

205 GPO – the General Post Office in O'Connell Street,
headquarters of the 1916 Rising.

206 gunboat *Helga* – the *Helga* did not come up the Liffey until the Wednesday of Easter Week, the Rising having begun on Monday.

– th' boyo – Uncle Peter.

shanghaied – forced into a situation from which there is no escape.

– Orange – Mrs Burgess is a Protestant and unionist, which may be enough to identify her with the Orange Society in Northern Ireland (founded 1794 as a defence organisation dedicated to that first great loyalist King William of Orange (1650–1702)). Thus, here, 'Orange' means 'loyalist'.

207 Sorra mend th' lasses – bad luck to the women (Dublinese).

210 only for – if it wasn't for.

th' tossers – the coins and strip of wood with which to play 'pitch-and-toss'. The men would bet on whether the coins came up 'heads' or 'harps' (tails), the two sides of the Irish coinage.

– oul' son – a friendly greeting, gender-neutral.

211 a juice ... a tanner – two (old) pence, and six (old) pence. Before decimalisation in 1971 there were twelve pennies in a shilling and hence a special coin for sixpence, half a shilling.

212 th' Volunteers – that is, those in O'Connell Street, who fired on the Irish themselves in an attempt to stop the looting (compare pp. 218–19).

213 Wrathmines – the fashionable suburb of Rathmines, its higher class designated by the fancy (British) pronunciation.

216 from backside to breakfast time – a Dublin expression: inside out.

– kinch – twist (Ayling, *Seven Plays*, glossary).

- sorra mind I'd mind – I wouldn't mind in the least ('sorra' = sorrow = strong negative).
- met with a dhrop – got a shock
- mot – girl (Dublin slang).

220 The Minsthrel Boys – the patriots. The reference is to Thomas Moore's poem, 'The Minstrel Boy to the war is gone', *Irish Melodies*, 1807.

225 shelter me safely in th' shadow of Thy wings – from Psalms 91: 4.

227 a nose – suspicion.
- pimpin' – spying.
- Danes ... Brian Boru – in 1014 Brian Boru, high king of Ireland, won a decisive battle against the Danes at Clontarf.
- Spuds up again – spades are trumps again. They are playing 'twenty-five'.

228 hand runnin' – in succession.

233 gone west – dead. The phrase was much used during World War I.
- sorrow may endure ... mornin' – a quotation from the Bible, Psalms 30: 5. O'Casey replaced 'weeping' with 'sorrow'.
- Lead, kindly light – a hymn written in 1832 by John Henry Cardinal Newman (1801–90), a convert well known to Dubliners, since he founded the Catholic University (later University College, Dublin) at St Stephen's Green in 1854.

236 a man's a man – echo of a poem by Robert Burns (1759–96), 'For a' that, and a' that'.

238 join hup – conscription was a controversial subject in Ireland in 1916, but was successfully kept out.
- Shinners – members of Sinn Féin.

239 redjesthered – registered (professional).

   – picaroons – thieves.
241 blighter – contemptible or annoying person.
247 They were summoned ... 'owme! – the popular
   World War I song by Ivor Novello (1893–1951).

References

Agate, James, 'The Plough and the Stars (1926)', in Sean
   O'Casey: Modern Judgements, ed. Ronald Ayling,
   London: Macmillan, 1969, pp. 79–81.
Ayling, Ronald, ed., O'Casey: The Dublin Trilogy: A
   Casebook, London: Macmillan, 1985, pp. 171–87.
Gregory, Lady Augusta, Lady Gregory's Journals, Vol. 2,
   Books 30–44, ed. Daniel J. Murphy, Gerrards Cross:
   Colin Smythe, 1987, 20 Sept. 1925, pp. 41, 42.
Johnston, Denis, 'Sean O'Casey: An Appreciation (1926)',
   in Sean O'Casey: Modern Judgements, ed. Ronald
   Ayling, London: Macmillan, 1969, pp. 82–3, 85.
Lindsay, Jack, 'The Plough and the Stars Reconsidered',
   in The Sean O'Casey Review, 2.2 (1976), pp. 187–95.
Lowery, Robert, ed., A Whirlwind in Dublin: 'The Plough
   and the Stars' Riots, Westport, CT: Greenwood Press,
   1984, pp. 30–31, 100.
O'Casey, Sean, The Plough and the Stars: A Tragedy in
   Four Acts [Acting Edition], London: Samuel French,
   1932.
– Inishfallen, Fare Thee Well: Autobiography, Book 4:
   1917–1926, London: Pan Books, 1972, pp. 176–7.
– The Green Crow, New York: Grosset and Dunlop,
   1956, p. 9.
Thompson, William Irwin, 'Easter 1916: O'Casey's
   Naturalistic Image (1967)', in Ronald Ayling, ed.,

O'Casey: The Dublin Trilogy, London: Macmillan, 1985, pp. 154–65.

Yeats, W. B., 'J. M. Synge and the Ireland of his Time', in *Essays and Introductions*, London and New York: Macmillan, 1961, p. 319.

Chronology of Plays

Note: O'Casey's plays were sometimes published before they were staged, so to give only the date of first production after each title might be misleading. Accordingly, two dates are given for each play. The plays are listed in the order O'Casey wrote them.

The Harvest Festival (3 acts), the only one of O'Casey's early, rejected, plays to survive, pub. 1980, unstaged.

The Shadow of a Gunman (2 acts), staged Abbey 1923; published 1925 with *Juno and the Paycock* under title *Two Plays*.

Cathleen Listens In (1 act), staged Abbey 1923; published 1962 in *Feathers from the Green Crow*.

Nannie's Night Out (1 act), staged Abbey 1924; published 1962 in *Feathers from the Green Crow*.

Juno and the Paycock (3 acts), staged Abbey 1924; published 1925 with *The Shadow of a Gunman* under title *Two Plays*.

The Plough and the Stars (4 acts), staged Abbey 1926; published 1926.

The Silver Tassie (4 acts), published 1928; staged Apollo Theatre, London, 1929.

Within the Gates (4 scenes), staged Royalty Theatre, London, 1934; published 1934.

The End of the Beginning (1 act), published 1934 in *Windfalls*; staged Abbey 1937.

A Pound on Demand (1 act), published 1934 in *Windfalls*; staged Q. Theatre, London, 1939.

The Star Turns Red (4 acts), staged Unity Theatre, London, 1940; published 1940.

Purple Dust (3 acts), published 1940; staged People's Theatre, Newcastle-upon-Tyne, 1943.

Red Roses for Me (4 acts), published 1942; staged Olympia Theatre, Dublin, 1943.

Oak Leaves and Lavender (3 acts), published 1946; staged Lyric Theatre, London, 1947.

Cock-a-Doodle Dandy (3 scenes), staged People's Theatre, Newcastle-upon-Tyne, 1949; published 1949.

Bedtime Story (1 act), published 1951; staged Yugoslav-American Hall, New York, 1952.

Hall of Healing (1 act), published 1951; staged Yugoslav-American Hall, New York, 1952.

Time to Go (1 act), published 1951; staged Yugoslav-American Hall, New York, 1952.

The Bishop's Bonfire (3 acts), staged Gaiety Theatre, Dublin, 1955; published 1955.

The Drums of Father Ned (3 acts), staged Little Theatre, Lafayette, Indiana, 1959; published 1960.

Behind the Green Curtains (3 scenes), published 1961; staged Strong Auditorium, Rochester, New York, 1962.

Figuro in the Night (1 act), published 1961; staged Hofstra Playhouse, Long Island, New York, 1962.

The Moon Shines on Kylenamoe (1 act), published 1961; staged Kirby Memorial Theatre, Amherst, Massachusetts, 1962.

Select Bibliography

Ayling, Ronald, ed., *Sean O'Casey: Modern Judgements*,
   London: Macmillan, 1969. A very useful collection of
   essays.
– ed., *O'Casey: The Dublin Trilogy: A Casebook*,
   London: Macmillan, 1985. A valuable collection of
   essays and background material for *The Shadow of a
   Gunman, Juno and the Paycock* and *The Plough and
   the Stars*.
– *Seven Plays by Sean O'Casey: A Students' Edition*,
   London: Macmillan, 1985. Note the glossary for each
   of the three Dublin plays.
Dolan, Terence Patrick, *A Dictionary of Hiberno-English:
   The Irish Use of English*, Dublin: Gill and Macmillan,
   1998. Very useful for students of O'Casey, whose
   language is often peppered with Hiberno-English
   expressions.
Fallon, Gabriel, *Sean O'Casey: The Man I Knew*,
   London: Routledge, Boston: Little, Brown, 1965.
   Written by a friend of O'Casey's who acted in the
   three Dublin plays and was later a critic and member of
   the Abbey Board, this has first-hand accounts of the
   plays.
Greaves, C. Desmond, *Sean O'Casey: Politics and Art*,
   London: Lawrence and Wishart, 1979. A biographical
   study from a Marxist point of view, which is quite
   critical of O'Casey's achievement.
Grene, Nicholas, *The Politics of Irish Drama: Plays in*

Context from Boucicault to Friel, Cambridge: Cambridge University Press, 1999.

Hogan, Robert, and Richard Burnham, *the Years of O'Casey, 1921–1926: A Documentary History*, Newark: University of Delaware Press; Gerrards Cross: Colin Smythe, 1992. An indispensable source for the reception of O'Casey's three Dublin plays, especially for the Irish newspaper reviews.

Jones, Nesta, *File on O'Casey*, London and New York: Methuen, 1986. Part of a series on modern playwrights and their work, this little book is chock-full of information.

Kilroy, Thomas, ed., *Sean O'Casey; A Collection of Critical Essays*, Englewood-Cliffs, NJ: Prentice-Hall, 1975. Some very good material here, not all of it in praise of O'Casey.

Kosok, Heinz, *O'Casey: The Dramatist*, trans. by Heinz Kosok and Joseph T. Swann, Gerrards Cross: Colin Smythe, 1985. An excellent study of all of O'Casey's plays: essential reading.

Krause, David, *Sean O'Casey: The Man and his Work: [1960], Enlarged Edition*, New York: Macmillan; London: Collier Macmillan, 1975. A biography as well as a critical study. The first great work written on O'Casey, this is still essential reading.

– and Lowery, Robert G., ed., *Sean O'Casey: Centenary Essays*, Gerrards Cross: Colin Smythe, 1980. A valuable collection of essays.

Margulies, Martin B., *The Early Life of Sean O'Casey*, Dublin: Dolmen Press, 1970. A short, challenging account of O'Casey's origins.

O hAodha, Micheál, ed., *The O'Casey Enigma*, Dublin and Cork: Mercier Press, 1980. A collection of talks given on Irish radio to mark O'Casey's centenary. Uneven, but some of it is excellent.

O'Riordan, John, *A Guide to O'Casey's Plays*, London: Macmillan, 1984. A useful introduction to the plays.

Schrank, Bernice, *Sean O'Casey: A Research and Production Sourcebook*, Westport, CT, and London: Greenwood Press, 1996. The most comprehensive collection of information available on writings by and about O'Casey.